MW00477006

T: Stands for Truth

T: Stands for Truth

In search of the Queen...
By
Reyna Ortiz

Copyright © 2017 by Transfusion corp.

All rights reserved. No part of this book may be used or reproduced, stored or transmitted in any manner whatsoever without written permission from the publisher, except in the case of brief quotations embodied in critical articles and reviews. Inquiries should be addressed to:

Transfusion Corp
TransfusionCorp@gmail.com

ISBN: 978-0692933572

Cover Model
Vanessa

Edited By
Alejandra R. Aguilar

Thank you. . .

"Oh, my God. . ."

I honestly can't believe that I actually followed through. I set a goal and I decided, "why not? What do I have to lose?"

To every person that I've come into contact with, who has unknowingly shaped me for good or bad. . . I'm grateful.

My mother who not only gave me life, but gave me life, I will always be indebted to you and your unwavering love and support. To my friends who encouraged me, who made me feel that my story was important, I love ya'll. Society, my biggest teacher, I loved navigating through you and your oppression. My biggest accomplishment wasn't my Transition. It was the fact that I was able to Transition in spite of your bullshit. To my whole family, all of ya'll, I couldn't have asked for greater people.

Julissa, my sister, my niece, my child. Thank you for proving the fact that I didn't have to give birth to experience the joy and beauty of being a mother.

The Girls, stomping through, living our lives unapologetically, ferociously, I have so much hope and faith that we will prove what they feared all along. . . We are power!

In search of the Queen...

Reyna Ortiz

"If it swings from North to South, its a boy."
The pendulum hung over the pregnant woman's tummy.
"If it swings from East to West, it's a girl."
They watched as it swung into a circle.
The older Puerto Rican woman grabbed it and
straightened it out.
The pendulum swung back into a circle, they looked at
each other.
"Girl, you're having a he-she."

My earliest memory is of me running around our little
apartment in the inner city of Chicago.
"This is my hair!"
Running, laughing, playing and feeling free as a child
should feel.
I ran up to the mirror, I giggled.
I had a long towel on my head, I tucked it behind my left
ear.
I thought I looked pretty.
I pulled the towel off to reveal my short boy haircut.
It would take a moment to absorb this.
There was a disconnect that I didn't understand.
I longed for long hair, it represented me, it represented
femininity.
I was feminine.

I asked my mother, "when did you realize I was different from your other sons?"

> Mom: "By the time you were three,
> I noticed you were so dainty.
> You were very timid and sensitive, like a little girl.
> People would always mistake you for a girl.
> "Que linda" "She's so pretty".
> I would tell your father "he is not like the rest of them." Your father would say it was because I babied you. "I completely understood and accepted whatever it was by the time you were seven."

I grew up in a beautiful Latin family. My parents Anna and Israel, my brothers Johnny, Israel and Ralphy. I loved my family and my family loved me. It was wonderful. We didn't have a lot of money but what we had was love and support for each other.

For the most part I had a pretty normal childhood, family and school. Usually on the weekends we got together with the rest of my family. Lots of aunts, uncles, grandmother and a shit load of cousins. We would run around all day playing tag one tag all, freeze tag, and any game we could think of. I felt I was a normal kid.

I didn't really understand the magnitude of my gender and at that point in my life, no one made it an issue. I found myself always hanging out with the girls or in the kitchen with my aunts doing what women do in the kitchen...

gossiping and cooking.

They allowed me into their space and made me feel comfortable. In my family gender roles were in full effect. The girls did what was expected, be girlie, play with dolls and learn to be a "woman", cook, clean and take care of the home.

The guys did what guys do. My boy cousins were boys, playing sports, watching sports, roughhousing and were aggressive. I was never into that stuff, it didn't interest me. They were all really cool, never really singled me out or isolated me. I just gravitated towards the girls. I got along with my girl cousins, especially one cousin in particular, Vanessa.

She was two years younger than me.

"Let's play!" she would say.

We would create our own little world of "pretty."

We got along so well, she totally embraced my femininity. She treated me like one of the girls. She had everything a six year old girl could dream of! She had tons of dolls, kitchen sets, play sets, it was like a dream going over to her house. I loved it!

We played dolls for hours, played with her kitchen set, cooked for our children and pretended we had husbands. It was fantastic!

There will be people at random points in your life, who will unknowingly shape you. Looking back, I now realize that she understood me and at the same time, it was like she nurtured me. Our relationship was beautiful. She was my cousin and my best friend, she gave me so much support and comfort.

The Great Eight

I was around eight years old when I really started to realize the way I was "acting" was, according to other people, "wrong."
Random people adults and children, would laugh at me and ask stupid questions like, "Why do you walk like that? Talk like that? Act like that?"
You're a BOY!
Up until I was eight, I really thought that I was a girl... I did.
At eight years old I started to understand that the world saw me as a boy... It did.
The bullying really started to hit me hard around third grade.

"You faggot!"
" That's not a girl, thats a boy!"
"Ewwwwww..."
"You're gay!"

The giggling, laughing, pointing and name calling was something I experienced on a daily basis. I gave no shits!
You pushed me, I pushed you back.
You called me a fag, I called you a fag.
You hit me, I hit you back.
I wasn't gonna take that shit at school or anywhere else. I didn't deserve it.

It was rough to have to endure this at such a young age, but I never allowed it to make me question who I was or how I felt.

At this time, most of the abuse was verbal and the majority of it happened in school. Not one time did a teacher or any school staff intervene during these harsh years.

I started to make friends, they were usually girls.

Martha: "Ray, don't listen to them."

Me: " I don't care, they're a bunch of assholes."

The girls that became my friends were the only people who were helping me, protecting me.

It was always my friends, my girls. I felt safe with them, they were my saviors.

I kept this all from my family. My mom would ask "How was your day?"

"It was good mom. I had a good day."

It hurt me to lie to her. I was a kid. I was kind. I was sweet.

It was hard for me to understand why people were treating me this way.

Why did it matter so much to them the way I "acted?" Why was it their business?

If they were ugly or stupid, if they smelled or were fat, I didn't push them around. I didn't care. Those were their issues. Why was the way I maneuvered through this fuckin school anybody's issue?

At this point I was living in fear and in shame. People were cruel. I was a boy who thought he was a girl. But, I never let anyone dictate how I felt.

I didn't care what I had to endure.

This is who I was and who I will always be.

I didn't feel it was necessary to hide or act any different.
I refused!
I was learning to be strong inside and out, even at this young age.
I was preparing for a battle I knew nothing about.
I was a young warrior fighting through an army of ignorance, and I was ready!

I just wanted to live like the rest of the kids in my community.
Life was already rough just growing up in the hood of Chicago. For the most part, as children we were surrounded by poverty and violence. I would come home from the craziness of the world to be with my little brothers. We had such a loving bond. We loved and supported each other. Most important, they never judged me.

My father worked, while my mom stood home and raised her four boys and took care of the household. We were poor. There were so many issues in my family that having a young feminine boy wasn't the worst of them. All that mattered was that my family supported me and treated me lovely.

Junior High

Junior High was a little more intense. Children at that age were dealing with more complicated feelings and emotions. It was obvious, I wasn't your average sixth grade boy. I was exhibiting hyper feminine traits.

I was me all day! I had a native two spirited look about me . . . very gender fluid. I was a pretty boy, who really felt comfortable hanging with the girls. By this time I had made some really great friends. They treated me really normal and I got to be myself around them. I gravitated towards what I aspired to be, girls who acted respectfully, dressed nice, kept themselves together, had morals, and were raised to be "ladies." I couldn't live as the girl I wanted to be, so I befriended the girls who represented me.

> Me: "I love your shirt, it's so pretty"
> Rosy: "Thanks, did you do your english homework?"
> Me: "Yeah, that shit was a waste of time"
> Rosy: "We're all walking to get some pizza during lunch, see you then."

I knew that this "feeling" wasn't a phase or something that I was going to outgrow. This was my life and it was only intensifying. Puberty and hormones were so present in Junior High. Girls were developing their curvy bodies. Boys were just growing and getting hairy. Puberty is an ugly, terrible thing!

I was in shock, my body was really doing its thing and I was trying to suppress the fact that I was starting to exhibit more male traits. I would see girls going through puberty, developing their bodies, curves everything that I felt I should've been going through. All the attention that they were effortlessly getting from boys, I was getting the opposite effect, boys were mean to me. I was growing facial hair, my body, instead of softening, was becoming stronger and more muscular. It was so hard for me to understand. Why was my mind in a battle with my body?

I had no support with this issue, no one I knew understood what a **Transsexual** was in 1992 or even what to do with a **Trans** child. Yeah my family loved me, but I needed more. I needed someone to step up and take control, ask questions like, "What can we do for you?" Or even as simple as "Have a seat, how do you feel?" My family loved me, but they were clueless on how to properly raise a **Trans** child.

Family life at that time was becoming more and more complicated.
My parents marriage was falling apart. So, my role in my family was becoming even more important. My mom was relying on me to help take care of my two little brothers. She showed me how to cook and clean. It's like she understood. She didn't make me feel bad about being feminine. In her own way, she embraced it.

> Mom: "Now, that it's evaporating, you put it on medium low heat. Cooking is about timing, make sure you taste as you go."
> Me: "Ok, Mmmm... it smells so good!"

Mom: "Babe, it's so important for you to learn how to cook."
Me: "I know mom. How do I know when it's done?"
Mom: "I'll let you know, start chopping the onion."

I loved cooking with my mom, it was such a bonding time for us. We would just talk and laugh, she made me feel so comfortable. My little brothers looked up to me, to help with their homework, make them snacks. I had to make sure they had everything they needed for school the next day. My older brother, Johnny was taking a different path, he was a gangbanger and a rough one.

Some of my family was heavily involved with gangs and Johnny was no different. The men in my life where super masculine and aggressive. They solved the majority of their problems with violence. They were so quick to engage in hostile behavior, that they were rarely able to verbalize their frustrations. There were domestic issues or issues in their daily activities where showing their emotions, was an ultimate sign of weakness. There was so much aggression!

On the other hand, the women in my life where amazing! My grandmother had ten kids, two sons and eight daughters. She was the matriarch of my family. What she said goes, no questions asked. My mom had seven sisters. I was surrounded by the epitome of strong Latinas. My aunts were loving, loud, tough and very family oriented. I really couldn't have been raised by better women. They totally embraced me, they loved my kindness and femininity. I had developed great relationships with my mom and my aunts.

People would say "Oh, you must have been raised in a house full of women." Mmm...nope! I had three brothers and a shit load of guy cousins. It was a hyper masculine family. My older brother and some of my male cousins would say things like:

"Don't sit like that."

"Why are you walking like that?"

"Stop being such a sissy."

"Man the fuck up!"

My response was usually "Fuck you! I'll do what I want!" I always stood up to them and any other guys who would judge me. I might have been a "sissy" but I was never a coward.

I didn't care, I wasn't gonna act like a "boy." Most of all, I wasn't gonna take on the roles of the boys around me.

My older brother Johnny was teaching me to stand up for myself, he would purposely start an arguement just so we could fight. A real "tear up the house" kind of fight. I didn't understand at the time, in his own way he was preparing me. He was toughening me up, even though he didn't understand me. He knew what this lifestyle had in store for me. He saw what happened to "faggots" in my hood. He loved me, but it was hard for him to comprehend that I wasn't like him.

Even after being surrounded by so much masculine energy, I loved and embraced myself as a "girl." I'd be in my room listening to music, dancing, envisioning my future as a grand, beautiful "woman." It was a separation from my reality. The images of me living my life, gave me so much hope for the future.

Sexuality and Attraction

At twelve years old, who I was attracted to was apparent. I was attracted to boys, not girls. But, not just any boys, the tallest, the strongest, the toughest boys. I was attracted to what the world would consider "straight boys." That's a huge problem when you feel like a girl, but you look like a boy. No shade, I was a beautiful, feminine boy.

Going into a boys locker room as a feminine boy in the early 90's was a nightmare. I was either being pushed around for being a so called "faggot" or I was being molested by groups of boys.

They would grab my ass and show me their dicks. It was so mind blowing that the same boy who was pushing me around in gym class was trying to molest me in the locker room.

I suffered in silence. I couldn't tell anyone about this abuse. I felt it would reflect negatively on me. I hadn't confided in anyone about my coming out. I was ashamed that this was happening to me. Coming to a realization of how men perceived me at such a young age was shocking. "I was a sexual object." I had to make a decision, how could I deal with all of this?
How was I going to deal with the physical and mental abuse I was experiencing? Now it was progressing to sexual abuse. So, not only was I dealing with my own sexual confusion, I was dealing with theirs as well.
I needed to learn what was so special about sex.

I had my first "real" sexual encounter when I was about thirteen. I was infatuated with him. He was two years older than me. He lived in my neighborhood. He was beautiful and I wanted him. He was the average boy in the hood. When we were in groups he was mean to me. He would join with the others and harass me, but when we had an opportunity to be alone, he was kind to me. In some way he gave me so much insight on how men really felt about people like me.

I learned at a young age, that I could use my sexuality to my benefit.
It just kind of happened, we were two teenagers who were exploring our bodies. It was a significant turning point in my life. Needless to say, I understood my sexuality before I understood my gender. Can you believe that? I understood that sex gave me control and power. At least that's how I processed it as a thirteen year old child.

Coming Out
Telling my mother at thirteen years old was a very important step for me. It was imperative for me to reveal this "secret". I couldn't endure it alone any longer, I needed someone in my corner.
"I'll write her a letter, telling her I'm gay." But I'd think to myself, "I don't feel gay, I feel like a girl."

I knew she was gonna support me, but I wasn't sure.
I thought, "If she has a problem with this, I'm outta here! If she curses, screams or hits me, I'm leaving!"

I started throwing random clothes and things I thought I would need, in my bag; a little blue bag with gold stripes. I would've left, because I refused to live with a family that wasn't gonna support me! I would rather live on the streets.

Me: "Mom, can you come here for a sec?"
Mom: "Sure, whats up?"

Before she could fully step in my room, I handed her my letter. I tried to close the door on her and she blocked me. She wouldn't let me close the door. It's like she knew something was up. She started to read the letter and she was really quiet.
I was afraid. I was afraid of how she was gonna react. I began to cry.
Was she gonna tell me I was wrong? Was she gonna make me feel like my life was less important because I wasn't a "normal" thirteen year old boy?
In fact, it was the complete opposite. She hugged me. We sat on my bed and my mother told me, "It's okay." I was trembling.

Me:"I don't know what I am"."What am I? In my head I think I'm a girl, but when I see myself I know I'm a boy. It's so hard to live like this."
Mom: "Baby, I've known since you were like three years old. I've just been waiting for you to tell me."
We both giggled.

At that moment my mom confirmed what I hoped, my mom loved me unconditionally. Why wouldn't she? I was her child, I came from her.

Mom: "I'm your mother and you are my child. I will always love and support you. I just want you to be prepared, this is not going to be easy. The world is not gonna understand you. You're gonna have to be ready to go against what everyone believes."

"I'm ready mom, I am."

High School

I was starting High School. I was excited and nervous, this building was massive. I loved it!

About 4,000 teenagers coming together. It was insanity. I wanted this to be a great. I wanted to have the "normal" high school experience. I deserve it. These four years were not going to traumatize me. I refused! I devised a plan. I said to myself, "Ray you're gonna make friends not with just any girls, but with the most beautiful girls in the whole school." I did just that. As a boy, I understood that for boys the way that girls felt about them was everything. I had no fuckin idea what this place had in store for me but whatever it was I was ready!

HAHAHAHAHAHA.....

That's a fuckin faggot... HAHAHA.

What the fuck is that? EWWWWWW. . .

That's "Gay-Ray."

Yup, that was the nickname that the community had given me.

"Gay-Ray."

It didn't bother me, I knew I wasn't gay.

My family were the complete opposite of me, especially my older brother and cousins. They had built a reputation for being hardcore gang members.

People would ask me, that's your brother?

People were shocked when they found out who my family was.

I would come home and my older brother would ask me " How was school?" I would usually say "It was fine."

"Anybody fuckin with you?"

I would say no. I tried hard not to get my brother involved.

For the most part my days were pretty much the same. I had mixed reviews from the students in my High School. I understood that it was probably confusing or extremely hard to comprehend. I didn't hide anything, I kept to myself. I was a hyper feminine androgynous teenager in a high school where I didn't identify with anyone. I wasn't forcing my lifestyle on to anyone.

Yet, I had a lot of friends.

75% of that school was cool with me.

They treated me fine, if I was cool with them, they were cool with me.

It was like we had an understanding.

15% of the school tolerated me, didn't understand me, but weren't trying to either.

I was fine with that.

10% of the entire school, 10% of 4,000 students, hated me. They were absolutely disgusted by me.

I would be walking down the hallway and get slammed into a locker, or someone would throw something at me. There were multiple physical altercations, but I had to pick my battles. It wasn't the physical attacks that bothered me. It was the laughing, the laughing that bothered me the most. It was very degrading and hurtful. I was trying to be accepted as well as physically express myself.
I was a person just trying to maneuver through this fucked up life, just like everyone else.
What the fuck was the problem?

Walking through that school I could care less what anyone had to say. People try to make you feel less than, when they're not dealing with their own insecurities. They too have their own issues.
Ok, so I didn't act the way society expected of us.
I didn't succumb to the gender norms. I was and will always be my own person. I fought vigorously for my identity on a daily basis.

My freshman year was a scandal. I had enough! There was this gargantuan boy in my math class. Who acted like he had a personal vendetta against me. I knew he would probably whoop my ass if we fought, so I didn't try. I dreaded going to that class, because every single day, as soon as I walked in he'd yell, "fuckin fag!" I would try to ignore him. So, he would throw things at me and taunt me. "You're lucky, I don't fuck you up right here." I would just look at him, and wonder what did I do? How could someone have so much rage against me?
He didn't know anything about me, he didn't care. All he saw was a faggot.

He was way bigger than me and he intimidated me. It came to the point where I really had enough!
I had to tell my brother, I couldn't handle this bully on my own.

> Me: "Johnny?"
> Johnny: "Yeah?"
> Me: "There's this kid..." As I tried to hold back my tears. "He's being terrible to me, everyday."

That's all I had to say . . . my brother was instantly furious!

The next day, as I'm sitting in class, my brother opens the door to my classroom and asks, "Who is he?" I turned and pointed to his big, ugly ass and said, "that's him right there!" Everyone in the class stared at the boy, even the teacher. They gave him the look of "Ooh you're in trouble!" I knew he was in a different gang from my brother's, which added more fuel to the fire. Johnny said to him, "bro I'll see you later!" Needless to say, we all knew my brother was gonna make an example out of him. My brother wasn't playing. He stomped, beat and bricked him.
Even though Johnny was confused by my lifestyle, I was still his little brother. Thankfully, that kid never bothered me again!
The bullying diminished in general from that day on.

People started to understand that my family wasn't gonna have none of it. School became just school. People for the most part left me alone.
It went on to be, what I would call a pretty "normal" high school experience.

I started hanging out and partying with the girls.

> Rosy: "Let's go out tonight? There's this party in
> Chicago!"
> Me: "Yesss, let's go!"

I was in full make up. I had my own individual look, it
was so much fun!
Sure, I dealt with minor instances of disrespect, but for
the most part, I maneuvered not only through my school
successfully, but through my community. I had
established a reputation of being that beautiful boy in
the hood.
My mother called me a social butterfly.
I was just enjoying myself. I just wanted to have fun.
And fun I had!
I moved around a lot usually somewhere between Cicero
and Pilsen. But I always lived in the hood.
I was surrounded by hood boys.
I think one of the best parts about growing up Trans,
well beautiful and Trans, were the guys!

> Cute guy: "Damn girl, you're sexy."
> Me: "Thanks, so are you."
> Cute guy: "What's your name mami?"
> Me: "My name is Reyna."

At that moment, Reyna was born! I mentally
disassociated myself from Ray, Raymond or Gay Ray, my
name and identity was Reyna from that day forward.
By then, I definitely understood my sexuality. Honestly I
really liked sex.

The myth is absolutely True, most Trannies love sucking dick!

And were good at it! Why wouldn't we be?

We have one, so we know what feels good.

We know what it takes to make it amazing. Like, cum on yourself amazing.

"Finding dick" in my hood was so easy for me.

Everywhere I went I was propositioned.

Guys would ask "Wanna suck my dick?"

If he was cute I was like "ok."

Sixteen, seventeen was all pretty much the same.

Partying, school, friends and sex. As a Trans youth in the 90's I was living it up!

But, being a Trans identified person and not knowing another Trans identified person really bothered me. Looking back, it made me feel extremely lonely. I felt I had to endure this journey alone. I had a friend whose older brother was gay. He asked me if I wanted to speak at a university about being Trans in the inner city. I was always trying to teach whoever wanted to listen about my experiences.

There she was, I didn't know at the time, but she was a living legend. Her name was Miss Ketty, she was an older Trans woman who was very respected in the community. She was on the same panel with me. Afterwards, she said "Girl, you need to get on "mones" you looking a little rough." She gave me her number and said to call her if I wanted mones.

Hormones? I had no idea what they were for or what they would do to me, but I wanted them. I begged my mother for days before she gave me the $13 for my first injection shot. I met with Miss Ketty briefly.

She gave me a hormone shot, but I really didn't understand the process and we were too poor for me to continue paying for them. It would be years before I'd see Miss Ketty again.

Senior Year

My senior year was a pivotal year in my life. I was seventeen years old **Trans** and beautiful. I loved it! I stomped through the halls in "full gigs," cats suits, heels, I was throwing it! I had a full face of makeup, it was great. I "carried on" in school. I wanted to give "the look," and I was giving "cha cha" "hood fish".
People loved it!

I hung out with beautiful Latina girls. So, I looked like a regular Latina. My friends at that time were amazing cis hetero girls and they treated me no different. During late night parties, they watched over me. If anybody had a problem with me, they had a problem with all of us!

My girls: "Oh, if you don't want her here then we're all leaving."
Since I hung out with beautiful girls.
Guys: "Nah, nah, we ain't got no problem with her."

I was surrounded by strong, beautiful, Latinas and I was constantly learning. Unknowingly I studied their mannerisms; how they walked, talked, laughed, flirted and socialized. But it wasn't just the girls I was learning from.

At this time I had sex with at least a hundred guys. Yup, at least a hundred.

I wanted to identify as a "woman" but I had the sex drive of a "man."

I didn't have the problem that girls had, guys didn't brag about having sex with me.

There was never a shortage of dick. Instead, guys were so traumatized about what people would say if they found out they were with a Tranny. It was really quite pathetic. They walked around the streets with this over the top masculine aggression. Yet, even with all that masculinity, they could never walk a day in my shoes. They had no clue that they, in fact, were the ones who were fragile.

There was more of a chance of violence, if I talked about who I was having sex with. It was a secret. I started to learn how to keep a secret.

I understood if I wanted to live in this community some things were not spoken of. I never talked about my sexual conquests. I was having lots of sex with "hood boys," mostly oral, I hated anal. I had become a professional dick sucker. . .

The sexiest guys, fine, gorgeous, hood boys. Latinos, White, Black, I didn't discriminate.

If you were cute, I wanted that dick and I was gonna get it!
Most guys didn't care that I was Trans. Sometimes I would tell them, sometimes I didn't.

I was overly sexual and not very often was I rejected. I usually got who I wanted.

I believe Trans women are so sexual, not only because we're overly sexiualized by men, it's our testosterone.

Testosterone is like kryptonite to a Trans woman.

I was also introduced to "pay to play" some men were willing to pay. Usually older men, married men. The first time I had sex for money I was sixteen years old. He was in his forties, he used to follow me around in his car. Trying to lure me in with money.

I was poor, they had what I wanted and I had what they wanted.

It was survival!

In many ways it seemed like I lived a double life. I was with my family and friends in school, but no one knew I had a sexual addiction. It started around fifteen or sixteen years of age. It made me feel wanted and it was a form of acceptance. I thought that all this sex with lots and lots of guys validated me as a "woman," but it didn't. It would take me years to figure that out.

My family life was rough, my parents got a divorce and my mom was struggling. My older brother was in jail. Now it was my mom and her three kids. We were super poor. We were on public aid, living in a tiny basement apartment, with no money for extras.

Poverty is a motherfucker!

I wouldn't allow my lifestyle to mess with school though. I wanted to graduate high school and nothing was going stop me. I felt it was important to graduate. I was proving a point. I wasn't gonna allow society to dictate my life or tell me that I was incapable of succeeding.

Sitting in my English class towards the end of the year. There was an announcement over the intercom, it was about nominations for prom King and Queen. Then it happened, a boy raised his hand and said. "I wanna nominate Ray for Prom Queen." That was it. The kids in my class all yelled "YES! Why not Ray?" My teacher was completely supportive. "Let's nominate Ray Ortiz as senior Prom Queen!" I was like, "oh shit!" But secretly I was so excited. Word spread like wildfire. Girls would walk up to me and say "Girl, I know you're gonna win."

But, the reality was that none of that shit mattered to me.

I was living, I was a senior in high school. I was openly Trans. It was amazing! I was already a "Queen!"

Prom was approaching and I was nominated as Prom Queen. There was no money for any extras . . . including Prom. I had built a great relationship with my Home Ec teacher, Mrs. Dorman. I asked her if I could use the sewing machine after class to make my dress and she said yes!

I went to the fabric store, my mom gave me $20 for the fabric for my dress, but I stole it. I had to, I didn't have enough money, not even for the fabric. I designed my dress and made it myself. It wasn't high fashion but it was mine. I loved it! Prom was getting closer and the excitement was growing. People were coming up to me saying "You're gonna win!"

I had no posters, no buttons. I wasn't advertising. I really wasn't sure how this was gonna go.

A couple of days before Prom, we had a dinner dance where seniors were acknowledged for their accomplishments. That evening I won best dressed (even though I stole all of the clothes I was wearing). I also won most changed since Freshman year (of course, that was a given). I won most popular student of 1998 (A Tranny? Why not?). I was so proud, because society needed to understand we are people, we deserved the same opportunities as everyone else!

The morning of Prom I was in our basement apartment. My mom was at work. I was doing my hair and my makeup. I was so proud of my dress and my look. I was so excited. This whole night, my little brothers were so supportive. Well, they were supportive my whole life.

> Ralph: "You look so pretty, are you excited?"
> Izzy: "Do you think you're gonna win?"
> Me: "I hope so! I'm not sure though . . . but I really don't care, I just wanna have fun! I'll call you guys tonight and let you know what happened."

I went to Prom with a group of my friends. All of my friends had dates and we were all dolled up. I had no date. No boy in his right mind, in my hood was gonna take me to Prom, but I gave no fucks! I didn't need anyone for shit! I had all I needed . . . me! Prom was so beautiful, so fancy. Everyone looked so happy. It was such an amazing experience. We ate, we danced. I loved it so much and I absorbed every moment of it!

Finally, it was time . . . time to announce the Prom King and Queen.

I had butterflies in my stomach. The whole experience was very surreal and I was so honored and grateful to have been able to achieve this level of respect from my peers. I was wondering if I could actually win this.

Our Prom King was announced. He was our all state champion wrestler, womanizer, and super popular, Andrew Pina. I had butterflies in my stomach! The announcement started . . . "this year's 1998 Prom Queen is" . . . silence. . ."Ray Ortiz." My group of peers erupted in applause and cheers. They were all cheering and applauding for me! Yes, it was hard to believe it, even for me! Looking back, I started at that school four years prior, literally fighting my way through the judgemental crowds. That night, I finished my high school experience gracefully, walking through a cheering crowd of the same peers.

It was an incredible feeling. I had earned their respect. Me, alone.

I approached my Principal who had my crown. I looked at her, she had a kind smile on her face. She placed the beautiful crown on my head.

I turned around to flashing lights and people cheering. Some of my friends were in tears. At that moment, at that exact moment, I realized that I could do and be anything or anyone I wanted. If you fight for what you truly believe in you can accomplish it! It was one of the most beautiful nights of my life.

I deserved it.

Reality

High school was over. The bubble of security that I had created for myself was over. It was time to hit the real world. Society really doesn't understand what a Transition is for a Trans person. It is in fact a change that takes time. Its different for every Trans person. We all have our own idea of what our Transition should look like.

Of course I wanted to be beautiful, with smooth skin and big boobs, but I couldn't afford it. Even if I could afford it, I didn't know where to start. Up until this point, even after high school, nobody, not once, had sat me down and explained anything about being Trans. After all of these years, I was still living in limbo.

Growing up, people just assumed that after high school I would go get my beauty license and do hair. Like that's the "go to" career for a Trans woman. At a young age I learned that I couldn't do people's hair. It just didn't get my attention. It really wasn't for me. I did the next best thing, I went to an overpriced design school in downtown Chicago and I hated it! This place was more interested in getting you wrapped up in student loans and debt, instead of furthering your education and career.

At the age of nineteen, I wasn't sure what lie ahead of me. I would think, "what do people like me do? Or become? Or love to do?" I had no idea, not even a clue about Trans history or our future. Then, one day a friend from high school told me about this "gay club" in the city. I had never been to a "gay club." So, I was like "yesssssss, lets go!" It was my first time getting introduced to "the scene" and I was so excited!

To my shock, people knew who I was. People at the club told me, "you're that Tranny that won Prom Queen!" I was getting my "life." People in the scene had already heard that I was a QUEEN! Let the partying begin! The gay scene in Chicago in the late 90's was amazing! Parties, parties and more parties. I was working, going to school and of course, partying!

I put my Transition on the back burner for a little while. At the time, it felt like a goal, that was almost impossible to reach. I would see other Trans girls "the girls." We were cool with each other but never really sat down and had a conversation. There was a lot of intercommunity confusion. It was like we knew we were going through the same experiences, but we weren't supporting one another. Instead, there was "shade." I didn't care. I really wanted to befriend another Trans woman, but it was proving more difficult than I anticipated.

For the most part, my life was pretty normal. I went to work as a teller at a bank. Yes, I aimed high! I would be considered an androgynous person at this time, meaning I displayed both sexes. People didn't know what the fuck I was! They would ask, "are you a man or a woman?" I usually just ignored that shit. I wasn't gonna feed into their negativity. Maybe, I just couldn't admit that I was clueless about the Transition process.

Feeling really frustrated with my Transition, I was living a very unhealthy lifestyle, having lots of high risk sex and gaining weight. I was just in a bad place. Like anyone else, my identity is so important to me that it affected more than just the outside. Not being able to identify as "female" was making me very unhappy.

I was twenty years old, when I received the most beautiful gift. At the time, I didn't understand the magnitude of this gift. It was life changing. We received a baby, a little baby girl. She was two days old, when she came to my family. She was given to us. My brother and his girlfriend at the time, weren't ready for parenthood. So my mother took full responsibility. I instantly fell in love with this precious and beautiful baby girl. She brought so much peace and love into our crazy household.
I knew that I would never have a child of my own, I had already accepted it.

Having a brand new tiny baby girl in our house had given me a whole new perspective on womanhood. I was up at all hours of the night, feeding her, changing her, loving her. It was the most beautiful experience. I was so grateful to have a chance to raise a child. It was like a dream come true. She gave me so much purpose in life. I was spoiling the shit out of her. In return, she gave me so much happiness. To me she was the most beautiful little baby girl. She filled a void that I never thought was even there. One of my biggest issues with being a Trans woman was that I felt robbed. I would've made an amazing mother! I would constantly tell her, " I love you little baby, you are so special to me." She became the absolute love of my life. I promised her "I will always do my best to give you the life I never had, but always wanted."

The Girls

One day my friend Juanita said "Hey, I got someone you should meet." I was like who? She said, "This **Tranny**, who did my hair. I told her about you and she wants to meet you."

I think my friend Juanita knew how much I wanted to meet another **Trans** woman. I was excited and nervous. I asked, "Really? She wants to meet me? When?" Without hesitation Juanita said, "Now! Let's go to her house!"

We get to her house, which wasn't far from mine. There she was in her full glory, topless and in her panties.

Her name is Monica. She was a woman! A **Trans** woman. I often like to say "I went to her house and never left."

She was everything I was looking for, she had a career and a husband.

She was living her life as it was intended, I was blown away.

This is possible. She gave me hope.

Instantly, she became my best friend! Or what we say in the scene my "Drag Mother" I had a lot to learn and she had a lot to teach me.

She was my first real interaction with another **Trans** woman, she was willing to take me in as her "drag daughter." I was being groomed and taught by the best.

I was twenty years old and I absorbed everything, every word.

I was in class and she was my teacher, my mentor. I loved her. She would yell at me . . . "You're not a woman!

You think you're a woman, because you were raised by women. You're a **T**ranssexual!"

That hit my soul, it was really the first time someone was actually taking the time to show me who I was.

It was magical!
Monica was part of a huge unofficial community of **T**rans women. Monica was actually the "daughter" of Miss Ketty, the **T**rans woman I met in my teens. These **T**rans women were beautiful, smart, resourceful everything I needed to absorb and learn.
They accepted me with open arms, It was wonderful! They were women like me, or who I aspired to be.

I would sit back and just listen, they had their own language and their mannerisms were something I had never seen. I was so excited for the opportunity to learn who I was. It was like a rebirth.

Everything I thought I knew about myself I had to relearn. I was a "community newborn."

They were my girls, my **T**rans culture.
After twenty years of battling and struggling to really understand what this life had in store for me now the answers were right in my face . . .

Body: The beauty of **T**ransitioning your body is that you get to design your idea of what femininity and beauty are. Surge: This is surgery, which for the most part is completely necessary for a **T**rans woman. It really varies from girl to girl, it's about achieving the level in their **T**ransition that makes them comfortable. Mones: Hormones, **T**rans women take testosterone blockers and estrogen to enhance their femininity internally. It's a very important part of the **T**ransition process.

Hoing: Prostituting, which leads you to understand sexwork. This can become a huge factor in a lot of girls Transitions. Boosting: Basically stealing or defrauding the system in whichever way necessary. Sil: Silicone, how most of these bitches got that boddyy! Medical grade and non medical grade silicone are available. It can be injected into that ass, tits, lips, face and hips. Most girls can go a lifetime with no complications, some complications, others are less fortunate and die. These are just more examples of the extremes that Trans women go through.

It all comes down to how you portray femininity. Every Trans woman projects their vision of womanhood.

This community had so much for me to absorb. It really was a whole culture of Trans women of all ages and races that I got to learn from.

People in my life were in some ways worried about me being introduced to my Trans community. My mother had sheltered me from this lifestyle, she herself was very sceptical about my new found friendships.

For being Trans I had lived a pretty normal experience. I was accepted by my family and by my "cis-hetero" community, but, it was imperative that I get integrated into my Trans community.

It was so much fun hanging with "the girls" we did everything "normal" people would do with friends. We'd go to the movies or stay in the house and cook. It was wonderful. what I loved was the fact that we all had different stories and different experiences to learn and grow from.

Most importantly we all had so many similarities. We were all fighting the same battle, the battle for acceptance.

It was all coming together I was getting the answers that I needed to further my life and most importantly my Transition. Now, I understood what we all had to endure in one way or another.
LGBT...
Hahahaha ...
"What a fuckin joke, they're always trying to silence the
"T"
That's what I was starting to really comprehend, that my community, my beautiful Trans community felt disconnected from not only the "cis hetero straight community," but from the "gay" community as well. The girls were standing on their own.
Where was the community support?
Where was "organizational support?" No one was trying to assist my community. These Trans women in the 90's were experiencing terrible discrimination, violence, and living super high risk lifestyles.
Where were the "organizations" that were getting federally funded grants to supposedly help the Trans community? Where were they?
They had a history of failing the Trans community, and the girls knew it.

Organizational presence, or lack of had created a distrust. The Trans women that I was encountering had become self sufficient. They were creating pathways for other Trans women to follow. They were finding hormones, getting surged, getting silicone.

It was created by Trans women for Trans women and it was remarkable.

The girls got their 'mones' from the streets, one of the girls would say, "here, take these, they're from Mexico, they'll make you beautiful. Doctors? Girl they think we're crazy, fuck them!"

There's this one place called "Joseph White" it was an organization that helped the girls get on hormones and most importantly get to see a Doctor that was comfortable with Trans women, but there were mixed reviews.

I stood away.

Even though I was becoming desperate, I would sit in a room at Monica's place with a bunch of the girls. We would talk about surge and about hoing. I was new to this all. They were everything I wanted to be. Beautiful, lots of them had already gone through so much to achieve a level of Transition that at that time I could only dream of.

I heard one girl say, "Here comes the fish, who thinks she's a queen." In some ways some of the girls rejected the fact that I had infiltrated both communities successfully.

I was working at a bank as a Trans identified person and that was a huge deal. The girls would give me props and say things like, "Yeessssss . . . you work at a bank that's sickening."

I had started to attack my biggest issue as a Trans person . . . my beard.

This was not just any beard, but like a SUPER BEARD!

My body hair traumatized me. I would jokingly say my father was part Puerto Rican and part werewolf.

In the early 2000's my first laser treatment was $400 just for my face. . . ugh.
I couldn't even fathom trying to come up with the money to laser my body. It was at that time almost impossible, I just wanted to be beautiful. I just wanted to live my Truth.

There were rules in my circle, you don't get your tities until you get that beard off that face. You don't walk around with titties and a beard, not in my circle! That was a definite no-no.

I was so desperate to achieve a level of beauty that I was comfortable with, but it was hard. I was working and had to financially help my family. My mother did everything on her own and I assisted with whatever I could. I used to hear stories of how a lot of the girls got their money through hoing and fraud. I was so naive, so naive to it all.
I definitely wasn't prepared for what was about to come my way.

Cynthia: "Oh, you work at a bank?"
Me: "Yeah"
Cynthia: "Let's have lunch mami, let's talk."

She was an older Trans woman and I kind of knew what she wanted to talk about, but I was still curious. What was even scarier was that I was desperate for money. The most important thing to a Transsexual, or at least to the Transsexuals that I was introduced to was their Transition. Get it done at all cost!

Cynthia: "Girl, I can make you a fuckin beauty."
Me: "Really? How?"
I was so excited.
Cynthia: "I have a plan."

Yes, I know, I had options. I could continue my life working and sacrificing to achieve the beauty that I wanted or I could make quick money. I chose to make quick money. I listened to Cynthia's proposition and defrauded the bank that gave me an opportunity. Before I had time to regret it, I said, "let's do it!"

Some people think they would've made a different decision. In reality, we're all capable of anything. Don't you ever put it passed yourself. Cynthia and I put a plan together. As she said, and now as I believed, I was gonna get every surge that I could ever imagine.

I wasn't thinking of the consequences at all. I was only concerned with the end results, the success of it all. I wasn't thinking of the possibility of getting caught, or what would happen if I did. For once, I wasn't thinking of my family, my niece, my mom, anything or anyone. I was only concerned with my Transition. My focus was only on achieving my Transition.

On a regular weekday, in a regular bank, in just a few minutes, we did it. I thought we had come up with the perfect crime, embezzlement and fraud. How stupid, people have been doing shit like that for decades. It wasn't the mastermind act I thought so highly of. I got caught a couple of months later.

I was working, like any other day, when the police stormed into my bank. An officer asked me, "Do you think you can steal $25,000 and get away with it?" At that moment, my life was forever changed.

Up until that point I had never been arrested. The officer grabbed me and put me in handcuffs in front of my coworkers and customers who knew me. I was embarrassed and in shock. I was booked at a suburban jail. My mother was devastated, she didn't have any idea that I was capable of doing something so stupid. I sat in a cell by myself for two days, asking myself, "What have I done? What about my family, my mother and especially my eighteen month old little niece? What about my little baby?" All I could think was, I was so brainwashed, not just by Cynthia, but by myself and my unrealistic expectations.

Thankfully, my family bailed me out before I could hit the county jail. My mom knew that identifying as a Trans person in the county jail would've been traumatizing for me.

When the smoke cleared I was charged with multiple felonies. My attorney was charging me $10,000 to represent me. I was completely fucked. My thoughts weren't about my Transition anymore. I couldn't help thinking that I ruined my life. How was I gonna survive this? It was a nightmare.

Months after my arrest, I felt that my life was falling apart. I lost everything that I had worked so hard for. I went into a deep depression, I felt hopeless. At that time, I thought I would never be able to recover from this.

Monica: "Girl, I told you that you should've never messed with that crazy bitch."

As I cried,

Me: "What am I gonna do? I can't find a job. My family isn't gonna help me pay for my lawyer. He's gonna drop my case if I don't start paying him."

Monica: "Well Reyna, when there's no solution. There's always prostitution."

We looked at eachother, and I knew what I had to do.

The Stroll

The first time I stepped foot on "the stroll," like the real "stroll" I was twenty-two years old and my life had made a turn in a completely unexpected direction. I was beautiful and young, but nothing compared to how desperate and determined I was to make that coin. It was very surreal.

I tried so hard to hold in my emotions. I couldn't believe that I had become a prostitute. Like, a real, street walking, prostitute. In the North Side of Chicago, there was a massive area dedicated to Transsexual prostitutes. The place was known as a "Trans hoe stroll." This was where men would go find Transexual prostitutes. The area was about a two mile radius.

The first night, I was terrified. I couldn't show it though. I had to be strong. There was a long line of cars. They would drive up and down the streets looking for their "perfect" girl. It felt like they knew I was the new girl. It was like they could smell me, it was very intense.

Yes, there was literally a line of cars. They were beeping, flashing their lights, trying to get my attention. There were husbands, brothers, cousins, fathers, even grandpas all in line to get their fantasies played out for the night.

My first encounter was with a black man, we call them "clients or tricks". He walked up to me and asked "how much do I need?"

Me: "Are you a cop?"
Him (laughing): "Nah."
Me: "A $100."
Him: "Damn, $100? I got $50."
Me: "Nope."

I walked off, my first client on the stroll wasn't gonna be less than $100. I was a "hoe," but I wasn't gonna be a cheap hoe.

I really didn't know anyone. I was on my own. I didn't care, I needed money and right now this was how I was gonna get it. I didn't know what this stroll had to offer but whatever it was, I was ready.
Jumping in and out of cars, I saw it as a business transaction only.

"What's up?"
"How much you got?"
"Are you a cop?"
I was really surprised how easily I adjusted to prostitution.
It was all about the money.

Deep inside I knew I had always been a hoe. I had always used my sexuality to get my way. This time I just got smart and started charging.

Walking passed the girls, smiling, nodding, saying "What's up?"
I wasn't there to make friends or enemies. I was there with the sole purpose to make money . . . oh, and not get murdered.

I couldn't believe how many girls were there just to hoe. On any given night there could be fifty, sixty or eighty girls, who knows.

There was a variety of girls, from "hard ass" Transvestites to "soft" Trannies that were so beautiful, they looked like they should be walking a catwalk, not a hoe stroll.

There were Black girls, White girls, Latinas, all walks of life, all ages, all Trans. There was just a bunch of the girls, hanging out, laughing, fighting, carrying on. We would walk away and turn a client and come right back to carrying on. We made the most out of it. There were men everywhere; on the street, in the clubs, some nights it was just one big party.

The clubs on the stroll were "unintentionally" set up for us to hoe. I would walk into a club with the intention of finding a client. It was an uneasy feeling, but clients were in these "Tranny bars" to find their "type" of girl for the night. They would buy their chosen girl some drinks, give her drugs and whatever she wanted. I didn't want any of that, I just wanted money.
I remember meeting this one client specifically, at a club in "boystown."

Client: "You look beautiful tonight. Can I buy you a drink?"
Me: "Sure."
Client: "My family is out of town and I'm looking to have some fun."
Me: "How much you looking to spend?"
Client: "I really wanna have some fun. Are you versatile?"
Me: "Yeah, how much you got?"
Client "$300."

I remember him specifically, because he took me to his picture perfect little house and we had sex in the bed surrounded by photos of him and his wife and family. I managed to get $450 off of him for "extras." I thought he was a monster for what he was doing to his family. At the time I really couldn't process it and I didn't have time to. I just had to move on to the next client.

The physical act of prostitution came secondary. The most important part of the whole transaction for me, was how much money I could get from a man. Some clients would try to be specific right away and describe what they wanted. I wasn't interested in those. Once I got that coin, I knew how to manipulate the situation. I gave the client what I wanted to give him.

It was so hard to fathom the direction that my life had taken. I felt that I had made a terrible mistake and this was my punishment.

No matter what, I had to make money. I had little to no options. I was poor, I now had a criminal background and I was Trans. My options were limited.

Soon enough, hoing became my life. I'm a quick learner. After about a month I developed a pattern. I figured out what days and times were more profitable to hoe. The best days seemed to be, Mondays and Tuesdays, Fridays and Saturdays between the hours of 12am to 6am.

My childhood friends were concerned. Even though I didn't tell them at the time, they heard rumors.

Rosy: "I haven't seen you in months, how have you been?"

Me: "I'm fine, just trying to get this case over with. You know, trying to stay out of prison."

Rosy: "Reyna, you're my friend, we've been friends for years. I have to tell you that I've been hearing rumors that you're prostituting."

It made me angry. I was in survival mode. I didn't need anyone to make me feel worse about my situation.

Me: "Look, I don't give a fuck about that shit. The only thing I'm concerned with is taking care of myself."

Rosy: "I understand that you're going through a lot Reyna. I just hope that you're not getting yourself into something that you won't be able to handle."

Me: "No one is taking care of me, but me. I will do whatever is necessary to keep myself together, I don't have to explain myself to anyone."

Being on the hoe stroll, is everything that you can imagine. I would take the train and get there around 12am. Condoms in my purse, a blade in my hand, ready to make coin. Imagine the complete desolation of knowing you would have to sell your body tonight to keep your freedom and help take care of your family.

This was my life for the next year and a half. I would sleep all day and hoe all night. I had to make the best of it. What's so bad? Every single night I was getting paid to have sex. I started to get to know the girls and even made "friends." I found that we all had something in common, not just hoing. I started to actually have fun. Why not make the best of your situation? We would be out all night, popping dates and carrying on.

Walking through the stroll one night, there she was one of the cutest little Trans girl I had ever seen, she looked like a normal teenage girl, walking through a Trans hoe stroll.

Her name was Angie. We crossed each other and smiled.

> Me: "Girl, are you Trans?"
> Angie: "Yeah."
> Me: "Oh my God, you're so cute!"

She was seventeen years old and a little beauty. We instantly connected.

We laughed and walked the stroll together that night, just getting to know each other. It was refreshing to finally find a girl on the stroll that I connected with. We became friends.
We were two hoe's on the stroll.

We would meet up at each other houses and get ready to hit the stroll together. She grew up in a family that accepted her, but like my family, they were poor.

Some families have so much going on like drug abuse, poverty, domestic violence, all at once, that having a Trans identified child is the least of their problems.

I remember one night before we hit the stroll it was October, getting kind of chilly outside. Angie told her mother she needed a jacket, her mother told her she better hit that stroll a little harder. When I heard her mom say that, I was shocked.

We were both kind souls in a cruel world.

One cold night walking down the street, having our usual, deep, enlightening conversations, that were only between us, we had a moment.

> Angie: "Girl, do you think it's always gonna be like this?"
> Me: "Hell no, girl we're gonna marry an old, rich daddy."

We both laugh.

> Angie: "I really hope shit changes Reyna, I can't imagine living this way forever."
> Me: "Angie, whatever happens with us, I really wish you the best in this life."
> Angie: "You too Reyna, I love you sister."

There wasn't a lot of positivity. We were surrounded by desperation and deceit, but I loved my sister and we were both just trying to survive. We were there to support each other, no matter what.

I wasn't ready to reveal this secret life to anyone. I was ashamed and embarrassed. I hid the fact that I was a prostitute from my family and friends as much as I could. I always held my head up high, and I was proud to work and help support my family. I couldn't ask for help from them and I definitely couldn't tell them that I was selling my body.

> Mom: "Where are you going?"
> Me: "Out."
> Mom: "Are you on drugs?"
> Me: "Nope, I don't do drugs, you know that."
> Mom: "Where are you getting all this money from?"
> Me: "I'm selling coke and ecstasy at the clubs."

That's what I told my mom I was doing to pay off my attorney and to help support me and our family. In some crazy way it was easier to tell my mother that I was a drug dealer than a prostitute.

In this lifestyle I was accustomed to keeping secrets. It started not to phase me at all. They were two of my favorite things; sex and money, combined into one. I was getting use to the stroll, I found it pretty easy. I looked pretty, I made money and I protected myself.

It was a cold November night, I was standing on the corner waiting for my next client. I could see my breathe. I was shivering . . . It was really cold. I had turned maybe three clients already and generated about $350 it was about four in the morning. I needed more condoms.

Back then we paid for condoms. There were no organizations out there giving condoms or testing options.
I was just another hoe on the stroll.
I walked into the convenience store and grabbed about three packs of condoms. I walked up to a short, dark, male, cashier.

> Him: "How are you tonight?"
> Me: "I'm good."

He winked at me, and I knew what was up.

> Him: "I'll give you these condoms and $80 if you go to the back with me." So I did!

That was just how it was as a hoe. Get that money by any means necessary. Once you take control of your sexuality, people sense it, and people are attracted to someone who owns their sexuality.

Walking through the stroll, sometimes you would hear. "You better use condoms like crazy or you're gonna die!" The older Queens would tell the younger queens.
There was only two things that scared me on the stroll . . .

The police was one of them. We hated them as much as they hated us.
They made us seem like we were the predators, when really we were their prey.

I was sexually assaulted by police officers on the stroll multiple times.

One night I was walking down a side street by myself. It was a perfect setting for hoing. There was very little lighting and no traffic. It was kind of a secluded area. He pulled up to me in his squad car and got out. He was in full uniform. He was a Colombian cop and from what I'd heard he was infamous on the stroll. So, I knew what was about to happen.

> Cop: "What the fuck are you doing?"
> Me: "Walking to the club."
> Cop: "You're a fuckin liar! You're a fuckin whore! I'm tired of faggots like you!"
> Me: What the fuck are you talking about?"
> He grabbed my arm and pulled me.
> Cop: "Turn the fuck around!"

He threw me against his squad car and was very aggressive. He was manhandling me, pulling me by my hair. He was "frisking me," trying to overpower and intimidate me, but really it was more like he was molesting me. And yes . . . a whore can still be molested. He handcuffed me, threw me in the back of his squad car and drove off. I was quiet. He asked me for my legal name. I told him. He laughed.
How many times have you been arrested for prostitution?

> Me: "This would be my second time."
> He laughed.
> Cop: "How much money did you make tonight?"
> Me: "I wasn't hoing."
> He laughed.

Everything I said seemed to be funny, but I could tell he was getting frustrated by me. All I could think about was how much I despised people with authority, especially when their authority was misused. He used it for bad, there was a deviant in that car that night . . . and it wasn't me.
After driving through alleys, I kind of figured I wasn't getting arrested.

> Me: "So, whats up? What chu want?"

He pulled over in a dark, really dark area, which seemed like he had been to before.

> Cop: "Do you want to go to jail? Or do you want me to let you go?"
> Me: "You're not fucking me . . . well not willingly."
> Cop: "Are you clean?"
> Me: "Are you?"

He laughed.
He gets out of the car. I see him opening his pants and he opens my door.

> Cop: "Suck my dick."

So I did, with handcuffs on and all.

> But, there was something way scarier than a

closeted, homosexual, **T**rans-molesting, police officer.

I didn't know much about her.

She was a straight killer.

She kept me up at night.

She would make me cry with just the thought of her.

She made it feel like our meeting would be inevitable.

Human Immunodeficiency Virus
The Trans Woman's Black Plaque

Why did so many Trans women die of complications of HIV? Maybe for the same reason that so many Trans women have to prostitute?

It's the oppression.

How would you feel if you walked down the street and people disrespected you for no reason? Or just made such a fucking scandal when you walked in public? Or feeling so afraid and stigmatized, that you would rather die than face the shame and discrimination by the medical system.

Some Trans women have it easier, they dedicated their whole lives to appease the masses with their beauty. They've had every surgery imaginable. They've become completely obsessed with every aspect of the life that they're trying to eradicate.

Obtaining that level of Transition, the type that some girls could only dream of, is a phenomenal accomplishment for a Trans woman. They go on to become an unofficial status symbol in our community.

That level of beauty works in our favor, either in sex work or simply in our daily lives. The more beautiful you are, the more money you make. The more feminine you are, the easier it is for you to navigate through this society on a daily basis. People will usually give you props and say, "Well at least she looks like a woman."

We overly sexualize ourselves. The surge, the hair, the lips, the body, all for what? For some coin? Not always, it's mostly to satisfy our obsessions with the perception of what we believe femininity is.

Most girls are less fortunate and it takes a lot more effort to be "passable." They might not have money to get surged or even have a little natural beauty, but those are the girls who really experience the hardships of being a Transsexual.

Young, White, old, Latina, ugly, beautiful, Black, Asian, "passable," "clocky," it didn't matter all Trans women experienced similar forms of discrimination.

One early morning, I get a call from Monica.

> Monica: "Get in the fuckin car!"
> Me: "Where are we going?"
> Monica: "We're picking up the girls and I'm taking ya'll to the clinic!"

I thought to myself, the clinic? Why the fuck are we going to the clinic?

> Monica: "You bitches are out there hoing, ya'll better be using those fuckin condoms! Ya'll gonna get tested!"
> Me: "An HIV test?"

I was twenty-three years old and I had never been tested for HIV. I had never had a "formal" conversation about HIV at all. There was so much hearsay and stigma associated with HIV, that we were so traumatized.

My stomach was in knots, I was terrified. I just sat there thinking, thinking about all the dicks and all the guys and all the sex.

In my mind, I was sure I was gonna die the certain death that has killed so many beautiful Trans women before me.

We get to a medical center in Chicago. I didn't know what to expect. I didn't have health insurance. I rarely saw a doctor, unless I was practically dying.

Stepping foot in this clinic, part of me wanted to run out. I didn't care I didn't want to know.

This was my life. The life that I valued so much, that I was fighting so hard to maintain. I was almost certain that I was infected.

Counselor: "What do you know about HIV?"
Me: "I know I don't want it. It'll kill me!"
The whole time I was thinking about my mom and my niece. How would I be able to tell them? How would my family take this?

Counselor: "How many sexual partners have you had in the last three months? "
I wanted to be honest, but I was worried she would judge me.

Counselor: "I'm really here to help educate you, to help keep you from being infected."
Me: "100, at least."

Even to say that outloud sounded terrible. She looked at me like she had heard this all before.

> Me: "I'm a prostitute. I have sex for money. I've been doing it for like a year and a half already. I use condoms every time, but I think I'm sick."

My eyes were starting to fill with tears.

> Me: "I don't want to die."

I got some amazing information that day. Information that I absorbed like a sponge. I was so grateful for this clinic. I was so grateful for this person who didn't know me, but cared enough to tell me things to keep me safe. In the early 2000's we didn't have rapid testing. It took two weeks for me to get my results. I had never prayed so much in my life.

HIV negative! Why was it so hard for me to understand that I wasn't infected? I learned so much and I was gonna try my hardest, my absolute hardest to keep her away from me.

> Monica: "Come over for dinner, me and Lexi are cooking."
>
> Me: "Cool, I'll be there in twenty minutes."

I hadn't seen my sis Lexi in a couple of months. I thought it would be fun to kick it. I got to the house. Monica and Lexi were cooking in the kitchen.

> Me: "Hey hoes, what's up?"
>
> Monica: "Were cooking caldo de res."
>
> Me: "Yesss!"

Lexi comes out from the washroom, but she wasn't her lively, exotically beautiful self. She looked sick, pale and thin. She looked like something was sucking the life out of her. It was obvious to me that she wasn't herself, but we didn't say anything. Why didn't I speak up? Why didn't we speak up?

Why didn't anyone address the issue in front of us? Why were we scared to offend her?

We were cooking and I kept an eye on her. Ugh, she was not washing her hands. She kept coughing on the food. I was a full time street walker who was obsessed with not becoming infected. I had a very basic understanding of HIV transmission. So, you know I was worried.

Me: "Wash your hands girl, what the fuck!"
Monica: "Reyna, stop being such a bitch!"
Me: "Girl, she's coughing all over the food!"
I gave Monica that look like ummm . . . What's up?
Me: "How are you doing sis?"
Lexi: "I'm good girl, you know carrying on."

I'm usually so vocal. I'm usually not type to bite my tongue, but I did. I just didn't know what to do. She was a real live reminder of why HIV is such a killer. We all know it's around us, but we're made to feel ashamed of it. Acknowledgement would be life changing.

I did something that I would regret for the rest of my life. I did nothing. I didn't even eat the soup. I'm sorry sister . . . I'm so sorry Lexi.

The very next day Monica called me.

> Monica: "You know what? I see how you are!
> You're the shadiest bitch I know!"
> Me: "Monica? She's sick!"
> Monica: "No, she's not, she's just going through
> it and you're not making it easier for her!"
> Monica: "You're the shadiest BITCH!!!"

She hung up on me.

I understand now, Monica wasn't mad at me, she was mad that she had no control. She knew her daughter was gonna die and there was nothing she could do about it. She didn't speak to me for weeks, until one day out of nowhere . . .

> Monica: "Girl, I'm picking you up. You were right, Lexi's in the hospital."

She picked me up. We didn't really say too much to each other. When we got to her hospital room, we found her mom and sister were at her bedside. We could see that she was fading away.

We were in the same circle. We walked the same stroll. We turned the same clients. We had fucked the same guys. She was in that bed. We knew it could've been any one of us. We sat in the waiting room, watching so many of the girls coming to say their goodbyes.

Suddenly, her mother came out of the room crying and screaming, "she's dead!"

I was shocked! I had just witnessed the death of a friend. How could she be dead? We were the same, or at least we came from similar backgrounds. She was twenty-one years old and she didn't get a fair shot at life.

Monica and I walked down the hallway. There were people everywhere, lined up, crying. Everyone was asking us "is she dead?" I could hear them gasping and whispering, "Oh my God, she's dead!"

As I walked out of the hospital, I thought to myself, Lexi, I'm sorry sister. HIV didn't kill you. It was our own ignorance and fear that really killed you.

Get it Together

That incident really opened my eyes. I felt that if I continued down that path that would be my fate.

On the bright side, my case was finally coming to a close. Believe it or not, I payed off my attorney all by prostituting. Now, I was officially a convicted felon and I was on probation for two years. Oh well, you live and you learn. I just added it to the list of shit.

There was just one worry, I still needed a job! I couldn't afford to get into any more trouble. Shit needed to change and fast! At the time, my sister-in-law was a retail manager.

Maribel: "Come in fill out an application. I'll make sure you don't have a problem with your background."
She was right, she got me a job at a large retail store in the mall.
I was so excited for this brand new opportunity, because I really needed it.

I wanted to escape prostitution. I got everything that I needed out of it for the time being. I needed a break from it, both physically and mentally.

One thing that I can say about hoing is that if you don't take control of it, it will destroy you.

I got a job. I was a part of society again and awake during the day. It felt amazing. I still didn't care about the stares and the snickering that I used to get. It didn't bother me. All I cared about was that I felt free again.

Once again, I put my Transition on hold. Don't get me wrong I was still a Tranny, I just wasn't at the level that I wanted to be. For now I was focusing on rebuilding my life. Despite any of the negative, hateful comments that I heard every single day, I was determined to not let them affect me. I would hear people say things like. . .

"What is that?"

"Was that a man or a woman?"

"Did you see that woman? She had a full beard!"

I was working a retail job dealing upfront with the public. Whatever phobias I had of the public and they had of me, had to diminish. I had to shove any negative thoughts deep in the back of my mind and focus instead on my job.

Giving up hoing wasn't easy. It's fast money and it was addicting, but it didn't matter anymore. My life, my health and my sanity were so much more important.

At my new job, I worked my ass off. I took extra hours, I was never late and I definitely never called off. All I wanted to do was work.

Thankfully, it all paid off, within six months I went from being a part-time seasonal sales associate to being an assistant manager. Yessssss! I was so excited. By that time I was living with a roommate in Cicero. Things were finally starting to look up.

Now that I was pulling myself out of the grips of prostitution, I knew that I needed to do more for myself. It was time to start getting my Transition together. I started by getting my beard lasered. At the time I was paying $250 a session just for my face. Also, I knew that I needed to start taking my hormones. Sure, I was taking them every so often, but now I needed to take them seriously.

One of my girls pointed me in the right direction, she said go to "Joseph White", they'll put you on 'mones." So, I contacted the clinic, but their first available appointment was three months away! I had already waited this long to get started, what were three months more?

Like with everything new in my life, I was excited. I really wanted to focus on my Transition. When I got to my appointment, I was nervous. I had no idea what to expect. I was told by the woman at the front desk that I had to see a Therapist. The Therapist and I talked for about twenty minutes.

He was a gay white man. I felt disconnected from him and his dismissive attitude towards me. I already don't trust people very easily. So his attitude just made me really guarded.

Him: "So tell me about yourself?"
Me: "We'll, I guess the easiest way to explain it is there's a girl trapped inside of me. She's fighting to come out."
Him: "So tell me, about how long have you felt this way?"

Me: "Ummm, my whole life."

I rolled my eyes. I really wasn't interested in telling my deepest issues to this judgemental stranger.

Me: "Soooo, do I get my 'mones?"
Him: "Well it's not that easy, you have to see a therapist two more times before you get your hormones."
Me: "What? Two more times? It took me three months to get an appointment!"
Him: "Well, that's the process."
Me: "That's bullshit. I know what I am. I don't need you or anyone to approve of my Transition. Fuck this place!"

I used to hate when people would try to make me doubt my life and especially my Transition. I know what I am. I know who I am. Believe me, I fought everyday for my identity and I felt that I didn't have to justify it to anyone. It would be years before I returned back to that clinic. I was not impressed!

The Realization

Work was actually going well. After nine months of being an assistant manager, I was asked to manage my own store.

While managing my store in downtown Chicago, I hired, I trained, and I fired. I worked my ass off just trying to run away from my past.

The girls that I befriended on the stroll continued to hoe.

They took the show online, no more street walking. They posted ads online and stood home while the clients came to the door. This was the evolution of prostitution.

Angie was still hoing and was getting her Transition together. At this time she had become, in the words of the girls, "a beauty." Stunning and surged, body and face. She was lovely.

At this point I had been working retail for almost three years.

I managed to get my beard off, but that was it. I needed more, I wasn't happy living in limbo.

Serious decisions needed to be made. Every aspect of my life, like most people, was in Transition. For a lot of people it's more personal, spiritual or financial Transitions. Trans people just have an added physical aspect of a Transition.

When I turn my back on hoing, I completely cut it out of my life.

It was like a drug, it always tries to pull you back in. For some time, when things got overly complicated I reverted back to prostitution. I used prostitution as a coping mechanism to help solve my life's problems.

I felt like everyone was passing me up. Most of the girls had completed or were completing their Transitions. I had enough! I made that call . . .

> Me: "Angie, what's up?"
> Angie: "Hey sis, whats up?"
> Me: "Girl, I'm over this working shit. I need to get surged! I want my breasts done."
> Angie: "Oh, shit! What's the plan?"
> Me: "If I leave my job for a couple of months do you think I can work out of your house?"
> Angie: "Of course sis! Then I'll call Ronny and make you an appointment so you can get your surge."

I was relieved and so glad that she understood me and was willing to help me out. I went to two breast implant consultations in Chicago; one quoted me at $8,000 and the other quoted me at $9,000. Dr. Ronny in Mexico quoted me at $4,000. Viva Mexico!

But this was only the beginning. I had to really think about how to make this money. Do I work for another year saving every penny I made to get my breasts? Or, do I post my ad and hoe my ass off and make my surge money in a month? Hmm . . .

I called Human Resources at my job the very next day. I heard of other managers getting sick and applying for FMLA. So, that was my escape. Thank you FMLA! Thanks to the Family Medical Leave Act I would be able to leave work for four months without losing my benefits or title as a manager. Brillant!

Surge

I knew nobody was gonna pay for my Transition. Not the government, not my family, not my parents. Nobody, nobody but the "Tricks!"

It was set! On the last day of July, I was leaving work to start hoing all over again. I needed a "break" from the daily grind, but I couldn't decide which job would be more exhausting.

After three years of hiatus, the bitch was back! This would be my first time hoing online. On August first my ad was up. An average ad cost around $170.00 a month. It consisted of a bio and about five pictures of yourself. Hoing online was completely different than hoing on the street. It was so much more comfortable.

I lived at Angie's house, posted my ad and waited for clients to call me. I think people have a problem with prostitution in general, because while ya'll at work about to lose ya'll minds, we're kicking it, laughing, smoking, enjoying ourselves. Everyday was a chill session.

We'd answer the phone and "pop" a date and just like that we'd go back to carrying on. Hoing gave me what I needed, when I needed it.
That type of hustle for a Trans woman is the equivalent of a man selling drugs. It's against the law, it's dangerous, but when done successfully it can change your life.

We orgasm and don't have to "recomp", It's all profit.

Once my ad was up, my phone was blowing up! My phone calls usually started with . . .

"Yes, this is Dalia, are you a cop? $250 for an hour $150 for the half."

> Me: "How much you got?"
> Client: "I got $120?"
> Me: "Oh papi, I need more than that."

All day long.

> Me: "Hello, this is Dalia, what's up?"
> Client: "Are you fully functional?"

I never really kept track, but I'm estimating that I had some type of sexual interaction with between thirty-forty men that month. Just like that, I made the money that I needed! I made about $7,000 that month. I was using $5,000 for my surge & expenses in Mexico. The other $2,000 were to live off of til I could go back to work. You might think this is a lot of money, but I know girls who can make that in less than a week.

I helped one girl count $5,000 and she got that from one client for just one night. When hoing works, it really works. It's all about how you absorb prostitution.

Like with any business, if you understand it you can be very successful. It's dangerous when you don't know how to control your experience with prostitution. It will consume you and eventually destroy you. I say it this way because I've seen it happen more than I would like to write about.

Hoing is not for the faint of heart. Most of the time you mentally have to place yourself in a different mindset, like you have to create another personality, an alter ego.

You were never alone, at any given time there were between three-four other girls working out of the same house. There were lots of drugs. That's how many of the girls dealt with prostitution, by getting fucked up. They'd place themselves in a different state of mind, smoking weed, drinking, and depending on the day . . . doing coke or "tina", any of these drugs.

I was always just a weed smoker, I don't like hardcore drugs, I never did. I would always say to myself "I ain't sucking dick for some coke." I wasn't gonna sell my body for drugs. I had other plans. Sometimes we would all get stoned, tipsy and talk. Talk about the shit, all the shit that we endured. The abuse, the molestations, the family rejection, everything.

Family rejection was a big one. It was the subject that would bring a tear to the eye of even the HARDEST queen. It fucked up a lot of the girls.
It created a lot of trauma. Some carry the idea of rejection with them everywhere. Family is suppose to be your base, your foundation. In all cultures and races, family gives you support, strength and structure.

So, what happens when you're rejected by your own family? What happens if you're told your whole childhood that you're wrong and a terrible abomination? Well, this rejection fucks you up. They're supposed to be the people who love you.
We weren't wrong for living. We didn't choose this life. We were dealing with the cards we were dealt.

On the other hand, It's felt good to both mentally and emotionally identify with people who have lived similar experiences. It felt therapeutic to sit around talking about our experiences and comparing stories. We had beautiful conversations, lots of them were very healing for us. That month I spent with Angie was literally life changing. She was my sister.

I made my surgery money and enough to live, party and pay for all of my extracurricular activities in one month.

I was ready! I was ultra determined to get this done, heal, recover and return to work living completely as a "woman." Getting to this level in my Transition was way overdue.

The reality of my past month was starting to really settle. I was getting nervous just thinking about traveling to another country by myself to get surgery. Unfortunately for me my Spanish was "less than perfect." It wasn't my ideal vision of how I would get my surge, but, I wasn't gonna get wrapped up in hoing again. I knew that if I posted another ad, for even just one more month, I would never go back to work. I would've just started hoing again and I didn't want that life. My objective was to make my money, get surged and go back to work. Mexico here I come!

Dr. Ronny was based in Mexico City. I had never been to Mexico or out of the country at all. I got up that morning ready to face change. I was prepared. My bag was packed, but it all felt very surreal. I grabbed my money wrapped it in plastic wrap and put it in my tuck (between my legs).I worked so hard for this money, I wasn't gonna risk losing it or getting it stolen.

I could see it all over her face, my mom was so nervous. I know she didn't want me to go but she knew how important this was for me and mostly how important it was for my Transition. We hugged, said our goodbyes and I told my brothers and niece that I loved them and I went off to the airport. I was ready to get surged.

At certain times in my life I've experienced paralyzing fear, but it's usually overcome by my extreme determination. Yes, I was terrified, but, I was gonna get this done at all cost.

I arrived in Mexico City airport. I went through customs and it was all pretty easy. Lupe, an older Trans woman who worked with Dr. Ronny, basically as his Trans liaison, met me at the airport. She helped me exchange money and took me to my consultation.

I was ready for anything!
On our way to the hospital I was enjoying the energy, culture and beauty of Mexico City. At the same time, I was in deep thought, it was like I was in a trance. I realized that I was willing to travel this earth, even alone and do whatever necessary to achieve my goals.

We arrived at the hospital and I registered. The procedure was all done at a hospital. People think "oh, surgery outside of the country who knows what kind of little clinic it'll be in." Nope, it was legit cosmetic surgery. I sat waiting for about 30 minutes before I got called into a consultation room.

There he was the infamous Dr. Ronny. He was a handsome, kind man, who thankfully spoke good English.

> Dr: "How big do you want them?"
> Me: " I want a double "D."
> Dr: "No, you don't have enough skin. You don't take hormones?"
> Me: "No, not really, every so often."
> Dr: "I'll give you 600ccs which is a "D."
> Me: "No, I didn't come all the way over here for a "D." I want a "DD"

He looked at me and smirked, because he knew the girls. He had surged just about every Queen I knew. He was responsible for changing probably hundreds and hundreds of Trans Women's lives for better or worst.

> Dr: "Okay, change into your gown, 'cause you're next!"
> Me: "Next? Like now?"
> Dr: "Yeah."

I grabbed the gown, went into the bathroom and as I was taking off my clothes, when reality hit me. I whispered . . ."what did I get myself into? Please make it through this." I live for my Transition, but I don't wanna die for my Transition. Once I was on the table, all I vaguely remember is tugging and jerking. Then, I woke up and realized surgery was a success. I was alive!

I woke up and I looked down. I couldn't believe it! I did it! I wanted my breasts and I got them! Getting "surged" as a Trans woman is just a small part of the Transition process. It shouldn't define us as Trans people. I've had friends who've had surge after surge like it doesn't faze them. I hate the process of surgery, it can take months. From the planning, preparation, saving, to months of recovery, depending on the type of surgery. That night I stood in my hospital room by myself. I was uncomfortable, but I was so happy that I had my breasts.

The next day I went with Lupe to stay in her home. If you paid $400 to stay with her, she would cook you breakfast, lunch and dinner. She'd give you your medication and change your bandages. She was really kind and nurturing. She would talk about all of the girls that she'd seen come and go. They would all come in with a dream, a vision and leave with a reality. It was wonderful to be able to have a conversation with a woman who had unofficially contributed so much to the Trans Community.

The first chance I got, I called my mother.

> Me: "Mom."

I can tell she started to cry.

> Me: " I'm fine mom, I got them. I feel sore but I'm okay."
>
> Mom: "That's good. Is Lupe taking good care of you?"
>
> Me: "Yeah, she's really sweet, she's always cooking."

We laughed, I just wanted to reassure my mother that I was okay.

I remember walking through her house on my third night. She lived alone in this massive apartment. I felt strange, I was heavily medicated and I woke her up and told her that I was ready to go home. She looked at me and said in Spanish, "No, te faltan dos dias mas mamita."

I felt I couldn't really celebrate my accomplishment til I got home. I wasn't comfortable enough to exhale. I wanted to be home with my family. On the fourth day I went in to see Dr. Ronny and he said everything was fine. My only question for him was, "can I go home?" He said yes and that same day I was outta there! I just wanted to go home and heal.

"Everything was fine."

My little brother picked me up from the airport, he just smiled at me and said I was crazy. My body was super sore, like I got my ass whooped.

My mom was at the door waiting for me to get in, we hugged and I assured her, "It's over with." We both cried.

It took me a month and a half to fully recover from my surgery.

I went to work fully identified as a "woman" and I loved it. I felt wonderful! My co-workers accepted me instantly. Some of my co-workers had really seen how much I had sacrificed for my Transition. They were all genuinely happy for me and it felt great to be accepted by them and society. It was always my goal to live, work and push through this society as my True self, and I did just that.

Love

Let me just make this really clear, I hate the idea of love. Up until this point in my life, I had sex with anywhere between 1,500 to 1,800 men. But hey, who's counting? Growing up, it use to bother me seeing everyone paired up. Getting pregnant, being "happy" or at least pretending to be happy. I was twenty-eight years old and I had never experienced this emotion we call "love."

I had given up on it. I figured it didn't happen to girls like me. It was just easier to be a prostitute. No emotion, they got what they wanted and so did I. I knew I was a good person, I had a big heart and I knew that I deserved happiness like everyone else. But how would it happen? Most of the men that I encountered only wanted to have sex with me. They didn't want to get to know me, they just wanted my body.

Because of the type of men I had encountered. I developed a huge misconception of commitment and relationships. I saw so much deceit in relationships, that I didn't believe in them.

My interactions with heterosexual men usually turned sexual.

At this point, I was working as a "fulltime woman." I completely stopped hoing. I was living in the Chicago 'burbs, in a basement apartment at my mom's house. Even though, the city was beautiful, I needed to separate myself from it.

It was hard to stay away. I loved the city! One day, while in the city, having lunch with my gay bestfriend, something was on my mind.

Me: "He gets out of jail in a couple of months."
Ronald: "Oooohh bitch. Did you tell him already?"

I had met this guy named Charlie years back, in my craziest times, when I was hoing and still fighting my case.
Back then, we hung out a couple of times, we messed around, but never had sex. I never told him that I was Trans. We were just cool and he liked me. He was everything a girl should stay away from; a troublemaker, drug dealer, gang member, in and out of jail, in other words, just my type!

What's the correlation between thugs and Trannies? The infamous odd couple? I would always say it was because of the struggle, we are the underdogs. Later it was bought to my attention that it wasn't the struggle that made our interactions so endearing, it was the hustle.

Charlie went to jail for a gun case. I told myself, "hey, if I got locked up I would want someone to write me, so I wrote to him."

It started off really innocent. We really just made it about getting to know each other. He needed someone and in some way, so did I. My life at that time was so chaotic, it was nice to even "pretend" to be "normal." eighteen months and a hundred letters later, he had become my friend. We really liked each other.

I couldn't fully confide in him, but it was so refreshing to get to know someone, and for someone to sort of get to know me. There were so many details that I left out.

I never told him that I was a prostitute.
I never told him that I was Trans. I never really had
many opportunities for a "straight man" to get to know
me, to get to know the real Reyna. Charlie was out of jail,
and ready to move forward with our "relationship."

> Charlie: "So when are we gonna see each other?"
> Me: "I don't know? Soon."
> Charlie: "Come on, let's chill. I wanna see you."

I'm a person, a good person, I'm far from perfect like
everyone else. But, that doesn't mean I should spend the
rest of my life by myself.
It's terrible that people can shunn you for just living your
Truth.

> I told myself, "I'm just gonna be honest and
finally tell him."
We were on the phone and he kept talking about hanging
out and asking why I didn't wanna see him?

> Me: "Charlie, I have something to tell you."
> Charlie: "You have a boyfriend?"
Telling anybody, especially a guy that you like, who has
no idea that you are Trans, is a really hard thing to do.
> Me: "No, I can't have kids."
I don't know why that came out first, but it did.
> Me: "I'm Transgender. I was born a boy but I
> now live as a girl. I'm sorry, I should've told you
> when we first met. I just wanted you to get to
> know me as a person. I didn't think it would go
> this far."

I went on this rant trying to justify why I didn't tell him from the beginning. I think I just felt guilty.

> Charlie: "That's what all this crying and fuss is about?"
>
> Me: "Yeah."
>
> Charlie: "Reyna, I love you. I think you're beautiful, smart and kind. You were there for me when everyone turned their backs on me. It would've hurt me more if you would've told me you had a boyfriend."

We laughed and a sense of peace came over me. All this time I was afraid of what he would say.

> Charlie: "So? When can I see you?"

I was at his house the next day. It was shocking to me. He was really kind, very affectionate towards me. I hadn't experienced this . . . ever!

> Charlie: "Reyna, I want you to meet my mom."
>
> Me: "I'm nervous."
>
> Charlie: "Why? She already loves you."

I remember my heart was racing. I didn't know how this was gonna go.

> Charlie: "Mom, this is Reyna."

A man had never introduced me to his mom before. It was nerve wrecking for me. Rejection scared me, it's what kept me in many ways from progressing. I was always afraid that people were going to reject me. She didn't, she hugged me and told me it was finally nice to meet me.

It was wonderful, his mother and I developed a friendship.

At this time I was working my regular job. I hadn't turned a client in over a year. I was living my life as it was intended and now I had a boyfriend, for the first time ever.

It was so awesome, we spent all of our free time together. He really made me feel so comfortable. He held my hand in public, he wasn't afraid or ashamed that I was Trans.

He would often reassure me and one day said, "Reyna, I just see you as a good woman. You're kind and loving. That shit don't matter to me."
It wasn't just talk, his actions spoke louder than words. I met his whole family, grandmother, aunts, uncles, cousins, sister and nephews. I couldn't believe that another family had taken me in and accepted me. They never made the fact that I was a Trans woman an issue.

I just wanted to move forward. I just wanted to forget about my past.
It was a wonderful time in my life. They saw me as a sweet person, a kind person. They saw me for the person that I really am.

Now, it was time to introduce him to my family. We had been "together" for like two months. My family was having a big barbecue and I invited him. I was so nervous. I had never introduced a guy to my family, but it went well. My mom, dad, brothers, cousins and the rest of my family were really cool.

That night, Charlie and I decided to take a walk around the neighborhood. It was a beautiful May evening. We were walking, holding hands, laughing, and kissing.

I was in love! Still, I just had to ask. I was ready to accept "love," but, I needed reassurance.

Me: "Is this for real, like for real?"
He stopped.
Charlie: "Yes."
We both laughed.

That was it. I was in a relationship and I was actually excited. I wanted to be faithful and encouraging as a girlfriend. He was trying to get his shit together and I was trying to keep my shit together.

We both had a harsh past. He was in and out of jail and gang banging. I was in and out of a life of prostitution "getting gangbanged." We didn't let our past affect our present, we both just wanted to be happy.

He gave me something that no man in my life had ever given me, comfort. I felt comfortable around him. I had terrible issues with men. I could say that I escaped prostitution unscathed, but I would be wrong, it created a terrible distrust.

For the first time ever, I had let my guard down. He knew things about me that I never told anyone, but I was so happy to confide in someone. We would sit up all night and talk, laugh, and kiss. We were inseparable. He became my best friend. I loved him. I trusted him. We had an unbelievable time and we really enjoyed eachothers company.

When relationships are good, it's a beautiful thing. When they're bad, it's a nightmare!

A year into the relationship reality started to set in. Both of us were experiencing different issues. He was, what you would consider a straight man. He hated me bringing up the "Trans" issue. Anytime I did, he would say, "you're just a woman, that's it!" He didn't wanna talk about it, ever. On the surface, that was fine, but in many ways it started to make me feel like I had to suppress all of my experiences as a Trans woman. I am and always will be Trans.

For me, being in a relationship brought out all these terrible emotions and insecurities that I never had to deal with. My issues with men were definitely apparent.

I'm not good in relationships, they bring out the worst in me. I was starting to realize that it might be easier to just be a prostitute.

Then, something that caught me by total and complete surprise. He cheated on me with some trashy girl. She wasn't even on my level and it was humiliating and so traumatizing. Here I was really trying to make this relationship work. I gave it so much of myself, my time, my energy, my "love," but all of it wasn't good enough for him. Not only did he destroy my trust, he actually got her pregnant. When I confronted him, all he could say was, "I want kids. I'm a Man!"

All that time I had invested was pointless. I hate relationships. I hate that we put so much emphasis on someone making us happy. That shit was terrible! Relationships are not what they are cracked up to be.

The damage was done. Needless to say we never recovered from it. We tried to hold on to something that was damaged and it was causing so much trauma. I allowed him to keep hurting me.
When it's time to let go, let go!

Soon after, I left my mom's house in the suburbs and moved to the city, on my own. I moved into a little two bedroom apartment in Pilsen. I was trying to move forward, but in so many ways he kept pulling me back. It was causing so much stress. It was so hard to let it all go. So hard to realize that I would be alone again.

We would fight so terribly, physically and emotionally. The end of that "relationship" was a nightmare. I just wanted it to be over and done with.

A couple of months after moving into my own place he was caught with drugs and a gun and sent right back to prison. Now there was no going back. I was back on my own.

Of all the traumatizing things that I experienced in my life, that had to be one of the worst. All of the hope, faith and love that I put into that relationship, was gone. I wanted it to save me, to save me from the life that I had. It didn't, if anything it made it all worse. It only validated the fact that the only person who would build me up, give me unconditional love, is me, and that was perfectly ok.

Rebel

I was single, living in my own apartment in the city. I believe everyone should, at least once, live on their own. You learn so much about yourself. Plus, you can do whoever and whatever you want. I did just that. Being faithful is for the birds!

Work was work. I threw myself into my job, so much, that it became routine and repetitive. After this long, I was sick of it. Working any job for seven years sucks, unless you're the boss or truly love your job.

I was grateful for the experience to be a Trans woman who worked her way up to management. It felt good to know and live that side of life, but it was so phony.

I was tired of working, tired of the corporate bullshit. They will use and dispose of you, once they had enough of you. I had my yearly review and I was ready. During my review, I confirmed one thing, people hate honesty. I told them how I really felt. Needless to say, I lost my job.

I didn't care, I wanted something different. I felt that I had wasted enough time at this place. I wasn't gonna give them anymore.
I finally felt free!

Fuck a job that you can't stand! It's one of the worst things you can do to yourself, and this is coming from an ex-prostitute.

I hadn't turned a client in years. When I give up prostitution, I really give it up for the time being. I can go years without posting an ad. But, when I'm ready to hoe, it's over with. It's like running your own business, you make as much money as you want.

It was different this time, I wanted to hoe. I had been trying to conform to what society wanted me to be. They want you to get up like a fuckin zombie and work a fuckin job 'til you die.

Not this bitch! I said "fuck it, I'll be a hoe." I was still living alone in Pilsen. So, by the end of that week my ad was up and ready to go.

Why do Trans women prostitute?

One, It's just easier than trying to find a decent job while being openly Trans. Two, because it's also easier than dealing with the bullshit and discrimination that we deal with on a daily basis. Three, money for surge.

That ain't shit, charging $200 an hour, even two good clients will make you $400 a day. You can wake up whenever you want, take a shower, get sexy and post your ad. Some girls get calls all day and night.

Think about it, publicly we experience discrimination, first hand. However, privately we are worshipped by men. The sexual objectivity of the Trans woman.

When a man is attracted to a certain type of Transsexual (emphasis on type) there is nothing you can do about it. She will be the only type that would ever really sexually satisfy him.

Men like Trans women for a multitude of reasons. I believe, it's that we project both feminine and masculine energy. This combination creates a very strong sexual energy. The man feels less "gay," because he can crave a dick, but when he looks up at least she looks like a woman. It soothes his repressed feelings of being everything he probably hates about himself. Blame society honey!

At any given time in Chicago, there can a hundred or more ads up. So when you get a client, in reality he's chosen you.

You are his type. A usual phone conversation would go something like this.

> Me: "Yes, this is Dalia."
> Client: "Are you functional?"
> Me: Yes, and I'm versatile."
> Client: "What's your donation?"
> Me: "$250 for the hour,$150 for the half.."

Functional as a Trans woman means you can get hard. Versatile means that you fuck and get fucked.

I never thought Transitioning into a woman I would have to use my dick so much. The difference between a woman prostitute and a Trans prostitute is really the obvious . . .

The dick.

Some men want you as the woman, hands down, submissive. Some men don't interact too much with what's between your legs. But there were men who would be furious if you couldn't "function,"

It's was a scandal!

We have the option to get penetrated or not. We can be soft and submissive or we can be hard and aggressive.

I was anything you paid me to be!

Sex with a Trans woman is everything you want. So much so, that men will pay a pretty penny to get him some.

But, not just men.

Oh, I started at $500 an hour for couples it was my absolute least favorite thing to do, but the money was outrageous! Yup, there were swingers, kinky husbands and wives, husbands and mistresses. I would just join their party. I was more sexual with the male, with the woman it was more mutual masterbation and some covered oral.

There are **Trans** women who are sexually attracted to women, but it's not my thing. I could never ever penetrate a woman. I simply couldn't. That was too much of a mind fuck for me. I'm not sexually attracted to femininity. I'm not sexually attracted to women at all!

People are so ridiculous when it comes to sex, but it's natural. If there's anything natural in this world, it's not the food, it's not the air, it's sex. Sex is one of the most natural acts. Attraction, sexuality, they make us fight the pheromone.

Why is it wrong to be sexual? Why is it wrong to embrace your natural sexuality? In reality, it's sad.

People are ashamed.
They're ashamed to say what they think out loud . . . "I think you're fine, give me that dick!"

Other than prostituting, my life was pretty normal. I cooked, cleaned, ran errands, hung out with family and friends. It's a very freeing career, but I knew that not everyone would support me. I told my mom that I had started bartending at the gay clubs and it was going fabulous. She was happy, and even said, "that's great you need a break from work." In reality, I was popping dates and it was fun.

Something I took advantage of was the traveling. I've never traveled so much in my life, like when I was a hoe. I would go to any major city and post my ad and make money. It was like a paid vacation.

I started hanging out more with the girls and they were usually hoing too. So, I would just rent out my other room and they would pay me per client. Plus, I had someone to hang out with in between clients. Sometimes it would be me and three other girls in my little Pilsen apartment just hoing. Making that coin.

Prostituting is really what you make of it, how you justify it. The biggest question to ask yourself is, are you prostituting to progress or prostituting to regress?

It always boils down to the same, sitting around with the girls talking about our experiences. I would make dinner and we would all just kick it, laugh, talk and smoke. At this point I was in my early thirties and some of these girls in my house were almost half my age.

They were beautiful Trans girls eighteen and nineteen years old who were traveling the country posting their ads. They were making money to get surged, to get comfortable enough with their bodies, so that they could face society and most importantly face themselves.

I was really happy to see how much my community had progressed. In many ways the girls were smarter and understood the Transition process so much better than back in my day. It gave me hope for the future of my community. The girls were getting on hormones earlier and getting surged earlier.

Monica: "We're going to a Ball tonight!!"
Me: "A Ball? Like a Party?"
Monica: " Yeah, I have someone you should meet."

It would be my first time at a Ball and I was excited.

A Ball is like a competition of different categories in the gay scene. Predominantly in the African American gay scene. That same night I met one of the most beautiful Trans girls I had ever seen in person, Vanessa, an eighteen year old Latina. She had been traveling around the country for two years making money and at the same time getting surged. I couldn't believe what a life she had lived and what a life I still had left to experience. That's the beauty about being open to meeting new people, you constantly learn from them. I felt like I had been through so much shit, yet my biggest lessons were taught to me by this little ambitious Trans girl half my age.

Vanessa: "Girl, Ronny "tried it with chu?"
Me: "Huh?"

She spoke that New York Tranny slang that even I had trouble understanding.

Vanessa: "You learned it sis."

She had this energy about her. I loved her right away.

Me: "If you're ever in Chicago and wanna work out of my house you're more than welcomed."
Vanessa: 'Really? Yesss, that would be awesome, thanks."

People think that we are weak, it's actually the complete opposite. Only a few can endure the life of an ambitious "queen." I have been blessed in my life to encounter such powerful Trans women. Trans women who survived and who continuously pushed through, tearing down barriers each step of the way. At the time I didn't understand it, but my little apartment in Pilsen had become a sort of resource center for the girls. They got life lessons in my apartment, that they would never receive from any "organization". Life experience is the best teacher.

Not just any queen was invited to my place. I was very selective on who came through my door. I wasn't with all the "faggotry". It was simple, act like a lady or get the fuck out! I wasn't playing with any of these hoe's, at the end of day this was my home and it was gonna be respected.

If I really thought you had potential to really get your Transition together, I would allow you to work out of my house. I would help you in any way that I could to make you a better person. Trans women need to build each other up. I wanted the very best for every single girl that walked through my door.

My landlord hated me, there was always so much traffic. Men in and out all day, every day. Clients or just fine, sexy guys that I used to carry on with, at all hours of the night. I felt everyone in my neighborhood knew I was super promiscuous or maybe they even knew that I was a prostitute. Whenever I was alone, I would just think about the need for more resources. What was in store for the girls? Were we all just subjected to a life of sex work? Subjected to a life of oppression by society? I felt that my girls were an extension of me, of my life.

I felt that I had lived a True Transsexual experience. I wanted better for my girls. I wanted my girls to be able to live freely without shame, without fear.

The Work

I was absolutely disgusted by the way my community was being represented, more like, underrepresented. There's people who talk about "the work", then there's people who fuckin do "the work." I got into doing "the work" for two reasons . . .

One, Trans women in my circle have been hustling and struggling for decades. I'm not just sharing my story, I'm telling the story of what so many Trans women are being subjected to on a daily basis.

This could just as easily be any of my sisters stories. Trans women are no longer living in fear or in shame.

The shit needs to stop!

We don't go through all of the troubles of a Transition to hide and live in the shadows. We Transition because we want to be ourselves. We want to live freely amongst society.

It makes me happy that Trans people are becoming more visible in the media, living and working. It's also beautiful to finally start seeing Trans faces in the public eye.

There's only one thing worrying me, what I was seeing wasn't a fair representation of my community. My sisters the beautiful, strong, resourceful sisters who have lived and died for our unofficial cause are still going through the struggles that we had to endure decades ago. So what was really changing?

Is it only gonna be "okay" for a select few to integrate themselves into society? Yes, there's a Tranny on TV, werk. That's great, but for every Trans person on TV there are thousands more, being persecuted for being themselves, it's fucked up. People need to really come to terms with whatever issues they have with Trans people.

Two, I was tired of prostituting. I really started to understand that I was so much greater than this fantasy, that I was subjected to by the same men who contributed to my oppression.

I deserved better, as a community we all deserve better. Sexualization of myself is undermining me as a person. I hated it! I knew I had more to offer. I couldn't give in to what society expected of a Latina, criminal, prostitute Trans woman. At this point I had been prostituting for almost three years. That made seventeen total years of sexwork. My body had been stimulated or overstimulated. I needed a new kind of stimulation, mental stimulation.

I really wanted to get involved in an effort to build up my community. I wanted to help my community on a larger scale. Education is the key to unlocking this oppression. I wanted to educate as many people as possible. I might not have had a "Formal Education" or a fancy degree, but I had so much. What I had was a master's in life, actually a motha fuckin doctrine.

I would go to these organizations to get condoms all of the time. I would give the condoms to the girls who would 'work' out of my house or keep them for myself. However, one day I walked into an organization with a different purpose.

> Me: "How often do the girls come in?"
> Supervisor : "Girls come in all the time to get condoms and to get tested."
> Me: "That's cool. I was wondering, how can I get involved? Are ya'll hiring?"

He looked at me kind of taken back.

> Supervisor: "Well, in order to work here you have to have an associates degree in social work or at least be a certified tester."
> Me: "Oh okay that's cool, what about volunteer opportunities?"

Once again, he seemed kind of taken back.

> Me: "Here's my number, if anything comes up I'm totally down. I would like to start getting involved with my community."

I went back home, posted my ad and continued to prostitute. It was just another day of being a hoe. The next day, I got up posted my ad, took a shower, got painted and waited for the freaks to start calling.

Suddenly my phone rings.

> Me: "Hello?"
> Emmanuel: "Hi, can I speak with Reyna Ortiz?"
> Me: "Yeah, this is she."
> Emmanuel: "Hi, my name is Emmanuel, I work for Project Sida. I got your number from my supervisor who said that you were interested in volunteering."
> Me: "Oh yeah, hi."

I was really surprised that someone was actually reaching out. It was amazing, but it gets better.

> Emmanuel: "Can I ask a question?"
> Me: "Sure?"
> Emmanuel: "You wouldn't happen to be the Reyna Ortiz who went to High School in Cicero and won Prom Queen, would you?"

I laughed.

> Me: "Yeah, thats me."
> Emmanuel: "I was a sophomore when you were a senior."

It was flattering to hear. It's funny how things come full circle. After talking to him I felt excited. We scheduled a lunch meeting right away.

I entered into this "organizational world" with one question on my mind, "what can y'all do for the girls?" That's the question that I have dedicated my work to. Fuck a fashion show or a photoshoot, we need resources. Trans women are more than estrogen and HIV. We have been pushed aside while we watched every other member of the "LGBT community" progress and

93

get their rights. What about us? Emmanuel told me about a project he was working on in the town where I grew up. It was the perfect place for me to start.

> Emmanuel: "I'm working on this project where we really focus on educating people in our community on LGBT issues."
> Me: "That's awesome, I really want to educate the public on what Trans women in our community are experiencing."

It was a match made in Tranny heaven! We both dove straight into the work. About two weeks later, we had an event! Mind you, this was all volunteer work on my part.

I was ready and so was Emmanuel! He was dedicated to our LGBT community. This was the best stepping stone for me to learn and it was such a great opportunity to be working with a such a passionate person like Emmanuel. He was investing his time and energy to help me understand the resources that were out there. I loved that we could openly discuss the options that would likely work for the girls and which one's I should be skeptical about. His experience, willingness to help and guidance really set the standard for me.

There was a lot to learn about organizational work. Whenever Emmanuel and I met with another organization I would ask the same question. "What can you do for the girls?" Usually their answers were hormones and HIV testing. I understand that decades and decades of institutional oppression weren't going to be solved in one day, or by just one organization.

Back at Project Sida, I started doing whatever they needed me to do, packing condoms, making test packets, making copies, filing. I was learning and absorbing it all like a sponge. Unbeknownst to everyone, my goal at that time was to become a certified HIV counselor. I felt it would give me an opportunity to really get some one-on-one time with the girls. Emmanuel was very patient, and I really couldn't ask for a better person to learn from.

Programatically I was great, I knew how to connect to allies, to people interested in learning about my community, but systematically I was terrible. I didn't even know how to send a "proper" email (I still don't). I wasn't impressed by the bureaucratic bullshit, rules that were unnecessary pissed me off. In many ways, it seemed that indeed the system was setting us up for failure and it boiled my blood.

I came to the organization with complete honesty. I openly talked about prostitution and my experiences. I wanted to educate, I wanted to learn what resources were really out there for girls like me.

Slowly, but surely, I started to understand that different organizations served different purposes for the girls. I started to learn how it all worked. Organizations get grant funding for specific "scopes," in other words, for targeted populations. However, throughout all of the organizations that I visited, I saw a lot of mismanagement of funding, resources, and time. I would hear about large portions of grants going to salaries and events and wonder why? Why were my sisters still homeless? Why were they still selling their bodies just to buy basic necessities?

I was looking for people who were truly dedicated to helping the community. Unknowingly, I gave people tests to see their level of dedication. Sadly, the majority of them failed. I stuck with the ones who I believed were in it for the right reasons. They brought integrity to the work and I believed in them, so I learned as much as possible from them.

I loved this work right away. It gave me such fulfillment. I belonged to no one organization, I belonged to my community. I spoke the Truth, no matter how harsh it sounded. I didn't care whose feelings I hurt. I was tired of the bullshit! At that time, I wasn't getting paid. I wasn't there to sugar coat Trans women's experiences or struggles. I told the Truth. Sometimes the Truth was shameful, even outright unbelievable, but I wanted everyone to know how neglected my community was. Everyone that I sat down with needed to know how my girls had been pushed aside for decades, by these so called LGBT non-profit organizations.

Then, I got to see it, or more like actually live it, for myself.

I had only been doing this work for about three to four months. I hadn't been to a doctor to see about my hormone levels ever. I learned a little more about one organization and how much it had "changed" in the last five years, or so.

I decided to give ol' "Joseph White" organization another try.

I made my appointment, I was actually excited to start the hormone process through a doctor. I was learning that it's important to get your estrogen and testosterone levels regulated.

Big things were happening privately in my life. My mom was moving out of state that month. After my appointment at "Joseph White", I had plans to a help her relocate and then start "my tour." Meaning, I would be traveling the East Coast, posting my ad and making my money. I had my trip all planned out, I just needed to get this appointment out of the way.

I got to my appointment early, I was really excited to finally get my hormone levels checked. To finally get on hormones prescribed by a doctor and not bought on the street.

It was cool, of course they test you for HIV right away, and I was negative. The nurse that tested me stepped out. While I was waiting in the small exam room for the doctor to see me, I noticed that the battery on my phone was dying. I got up to find a socket and found one in between the exam table and wall, so I plugged my phone in.

I stumbled and lost my footing. I'm not sure what I stumbled on, or whatever was in my way, but I fuckin fell. I fuckin fell on my fuckin wrist, I felt it shatter instantly!

I couldn't believe it, couldn't believe this had just happened to me. What came next was even more unbelievable. I remember standing up looking at my wrist thinking, "Oh my God. This did not just happen to me!" In my mind I was yelling, OH MY GOD! My mom, my trip, my tour, my life.
The first person who came to my "aid" was a male employee who heard me scream.

Employee: "What happened? Are you ok?"
Me: "Oh My God. I fell!!!!!"

The employee ran out of the office without saying
another word and went to get "help." Instead of bringing
the doctor, he brought in the organization's attorney. I
couldn't believe it, an attorney over a doctor? Why? My
mind was such a blurr. I still hadn't processed what had
just happened, when the attorney started talking. This
was before a doctor even walked in.

Attorney: "Don't worry darling, we're gonna get
you some help."
Doctor: "What happened?"

I was in shock, I couldn't verbalize what had just
happened. In my mind all that I could ask myself was,
how could this have happened? I try to be so careful in
all aspects of my life. I had come to terms with the idea
that no one would help me, except me. I'm the only
person who takes care of me, what am I gonna do?
My thoughts were interrupted by the doctor talking.

Doctor: "We're calling a cab and were sending
you straight to the hospital. Here are some of
our insurance forms to show the registration
desk."
She handed me ten dollars.
Doctor: "Make sure you take the cab, don't try to
take the bus."

Like I was interested in pocketing $7.50! I felt like they couldn't wait to get rid of me. I was rushed out of the office. I felt and saw darkness rush through my veins. I wasn't feeling pain, anger was the only thing I was feeling. Yes, they called me a cab, instead of an ambulance. Even though an ambulance really couldn't have done much for me, it was the principle.

I've seen people carried off in an ambulance for stupid reasons like being too drunk, or having a panic attack. I had no choice, I jumped into the cab that they called for me.

At the same time, I was calling my mother screaming! I was so furious and hurt.

> Me: "Mom, I was at my appointment and I fell. My wrist, it's broken! NO!!!!!!
> Mom: "What? What happened?"

I got to the hospital and walked into the emergency room and the lady at the registration desk says, "How can I help you sir?" She did, she called me sir. By this time I was in attack mode, I screamed at her, "YOU FUCKIN BITCH! DO I LOOK LIKE A FUCKIN SIR TO YOU?" The Trans women that I know are sick and tired of this disrespectful ass attitude we get from some people. Most people think that we exaggerate how people disrespect us, but it's real.

She sat back, I meant business and she was fucking with the wrong Tranny! I let her have it, "Who the fuck are you talking to? I didn't get all this fuckin surge for you to call me sir!"

Her co-worker intervened and started apologizing for her. I was a victim that day, in so many ways. That day I experienced a level of trauma that I wouldn't wish on anyone. I felt terribly scorned by everyone around me. While I was getting my x-rays the technician said, "Well, I'm not a doctor but you're gonna need surgery. That wrist is shattered."

I cried, I was devastated. I was a full time prostitute trying to take care of myself and my family. What was I supposed to do? As planned, my mom left, the next day, without me. She couldn't delay her move.

I had to endure this all on my own.
Dealing with this multi-million dollar organization was not gonna be easy and I knew it. I was injured, they called a couple of times to check on me and all they told me was they were gonna take care of everything . . . what a lie that was! Once again, they were dismissing me.

A week later, I had to have surgery. This was no small surgery, 100 stitches, six screws and a plate in my wrist. A nine inch lighting bolt scar left behind on my wrist. It was a travesty. I had $50,000 worth of overpriced surgery that I was now being sued for. All of this because I wanted some legal hormones? Coming back to this organization, turned out to be a terrible mistake.

Of course, I had to get an attorney. I couldn't prostitute. How could I even afford an attorney? As a result, I had to get some bullshit ass attorney who wasn't really interested in my case. I felt like both, the organization and the law firm looked at me as a bottom feeder, a scumbag Trans Latina looking to take advantage of the system. I truly felt discriminated.

This was discrimination at its finest. Everything that I hated about organizations and the justice system was proving to be True. Since I couldn't afford an amazing attorney, they dicked me around like crazy. I had one of those TV attorneys. You know, the type you see on TV getting people $100,000 for being hit by an automatic sliding door and that type of bullshit. Except, my TV attorney didn't give a fuck and it was very obvious.

> Attorney: "Yeah, you fell, no one saw you fall."
> Me: "I came into that organization feeling excited, I left in shambles. I didn't do this to myself! I fell and now I'm being treated like I did this shit on purpose! This is fucked up!"
> Attorney: "The organization is saying that this is your fault."
> Me: "Can I be honest? I think this justice system is a fuckin joke and it doesn't work for everybody."

He laughed.

> Attorney: "You could be right."
> Me: "They fucked with the wrong Tranny! I'm not gonna lay here like a fuckin dog and let them treat me any way they want . . . justice will be served in some way, shape or form!"

It was a cold February and I needed money. Try prostituting with 100 stitches and a metal plate in your wrist! I was very fortunate to have built a strong foundation of clients that I saw on a regular basis. They were good to me. One day, right after my surgery,

I was sitting in my room with one of my regulars who was the epitome of the perfect Tranny client and I was appreciative. He's been around for at least twenty-five years and he's been passed down from girl to girl. He probably invested more money into the Trans community, than any fully funded organization ever will. He loves Trans women and treats us respectfully. In some way he understands the complications of being a Trans woman. Those same complications are the reasons why he will always have to fetishize Trans women. Luckily, I was still able to make my money. If I could survive this, I honestly could survive anything.

I told myself, "This is all a test Reyna, you can do this."

This experience assured me that the path I was on, working for my community was completely necessary. We as Trans women of color are in dire need of help darlings. Almost every hardship that you can imagine living as a Trans woman in this society is completely True.

This attorney and organization opened the wrath of Reyna Ortiz. I fought my whole fuckin life, my whole life I fought for my survival. I survived the streets. I'd be damned to let this defeat me or challenge my spirit.

This level of discrimination lit the fuel for the fire that was now my motivation to shine light on the way we are mistreated.

Not only was I in the pursuit of understanding the disconnect between organizations and Trans women. I had experienced the ultimate betrayal and now I had the scar to prove it!

Of all my situations, this situation changed me!

Needless to say, my case was dismissed. They decided to throw $4,000 at me to shut the fuck up. My medical bills totalled $50,000. I healed physically, but mentally and spiritually I had some work to do.

I came back to work at Project Sida with full force. By now, I was hired to do contractual outreach work. I was making $300 a month. That's right, $300 a month. So I still had to hoe. It really wasn't about the money, I was on a mission and I was still learning.

One of the first projects that I helped put together was a focus group with about ten Trans women. It was very successful. We sat around openly discussing the issues that were affecting our community, like family rejection, prostitution, discrimination in the workforce, housing discrimination, institutional oppression, lack of medical resources, legal issues, physical and emotional abuse. This information was transcripted into a report, to be used later to gather resources. It was a phenomenal step in the right direction.

After the success of that focus group, I was offered a part time position at Project Sida as an Outreach Worker. My job was to find "the girls" and offer them resources that would make their lives easier. I had to find the girls in the clubs, on the streets, at the store, on the bus, using social media, basically anywhere and by any means necessary!
That's exactly what I did.

I felt happy, I knew that I got into this work to help build community. Instead of an Outreach Worker, I called myself a "Trans Resource Navigator". I gave myself that title because it was exactly what I was doing.

Finding the necessary resources like housing for homeless Trans identified people, finding legal assistance for their name and document changes. Finding doctors that were Trans friendly and connecting the girls to health insurance. There are a lot of resources available, but many of the girls had no idea.

Emmanuel and I put together an event at the local library, to release and discuss the findings of our focus group. I stood in front of a large audience and co-facilitated this event discussing the issues that were affecting our community.

Do you ever feel that energy, the spirits or God put people in your path for a particular reason? I honestly do.

Her name is Dr Bell, that night we were both on the same panel. Talking about my community, in such an enlightening way. I was totally blown away not only by her knowledge of our community, but by her compassion. The Truth and knowledge that she was speaking was just awe-inspiring and brilliant. We looked at each other, she reached over and handed me her card and said, "call me." She was not just an African American doctor who worked at the county hospital. She was so much more, she was an absolute powerhouse in the Trans community. Of course, I couldn't wait to connect with her. She was really the link that I was looking for. She was a doctor who understood the girls.

Together, Emmanuel and I organized a small event to present resources to the girls that we had connected with. We invited Dr. Bell who showed up with some of her staff. The resources that were being combined were really beneficial and long overdue.

I started to understand that she did everything that the other organizations did, but better.

Outreaching became a whole lot more effective. We made flyers in English and Spanish to pass out to the girls. I really wanted to get these girls connected to the resources. It was almost unbelievable to me that we had finally found a brilliant doctor that the girls could connect with in so many ways.

Within a couple of months, I was working for Dr. Bell. Project Sida had lost the majority of its funding and was partially closed down. She ran an organization on the West Side of Chicago. A safe space where youth were given an opportunity to express themselves without judgement or ridicule.

Tucked away from the wealth and lights of downtown, or the entitlement of the north side, stood the only LGBT organization deep in heart of the West Side of Chicago.

Dr. Bell was not only a pediatric doctor at the county hospital. In her spare time she put her heart and soul into this organization and drop-in center. This was an area where no other organization dared to step foot. Being connected to the county hospital, she was able to provide a limitless amount of resources to gay, lesbian and Transgender youths. Without her these youths were not likely to see a doctor on a regular basis. Some of the youth she helps include those who are HIV positive, homeless or just so disenfranchised that they have set their own health aside to focus on just basic survival.

They call the drop-in center, The Vogue School. At any given time this center can have between forty-sixty youth vogueing and coming to access available resources. Dr Bell gave me opportunities to learn and I became an outreach worker.

She really believed in the work that we were doing and best of all, she believed in me. She became my mentor and I didn't want to disappoint her.

I have so much love and respect for her. She's one of the most remarkable people I've ever encountered. She often encouraged me by saying things like, "Reyna, you're a lot smarter than you think you are."

I was a proud Latina Transsexual working in an all Black non-profit organization. I had never really taken the time to understand Black gay culture and it was eye opening

The first day I walked into the drop-in center, which resembled a small banquet hall, it was hot as hell! It had no air conditioning, but it was like stepping into a dance school.

It was The Vogue School . . . vogue? I had never really understood the concept of voguing. It's an art. It's a form of dance expression at it's finest. It's beautiful and powerful. I was fortunate enough to be in a room full of voguers! At least fifty youth were regulars at this drop-in center, where all they did here was hard core voguing. This jewel was deep in the West Side of Chicago.

It was almost unimaginable and at the same time breathtaking. There was so much raw, incredible talent, that I instantly fell in love with this place!

One thing about the right organization is that they invest in your knowledge. They want their staff to learn. Dr. Bell insisted that we further our education any way possible. She would stop you in the hallway and quiz you with a question pertaining to work. I loved it and I was so grateful for this opportunity.

This all went back to my youth. I always wanted someone to invest in my mind, not my body. Education was never pushed upon me, it was just "whatever you could bring to the table." At this organization, I had an opportunity to learn. Whether it was about STD's or HIV, I took every course that was thrown at me.

HIV and I had a history together, I went from not knowing anything about HIV to having a deep respect for a terrible, yet ingenious virus. Twenty years of sexwork, about 3,000 sexual encounters and I still managed to stay uninfected.

I saw it as an accomplishment.

I remember walking up and down the stroll as a young, lost prostitute. In many ways I understood how it felt to be stalked by HIV, I wanted to start helping and talking with my sisters about HIV prevention. I could've never imagined that I would be doing this type of work.

Especially after finally becoming a certified HIV counselor, a youth couldn't walk by me without getting tested. I not only wanted to test them, I wanted to do so much more. I wanted to get to know them, conversate, laugh, share my experiences and knowledge while they got to know me. Talking with gay youth and Trans women about HIV prevention was everything I wanted.

I was very blunt and would ask them, "are you hoing?" I wanted to be realistic. Since I could relate to the girls struggles and now I had some solutions to offer, I wanted them to trust me. It was very healing to be able to help.

I was trying to get out of sex work completely, which was proving to be difficult. I was and will always be addicted to prostitution. So, it felt very hypocritical to talk to youth about high risk behavior when I was still engaging in it myself. I use to counsel youth on HIV, then go home and post my ad. It became easy money. I'd have sex with multiple clients. Poverty is hard to escape and I was in a grip, a tight grip.

On the other hand, my work in the community became so essential to my daily life. I am working for two large organizations with the sole purpose of helping my Trans community. I believe in the organizations that I work for and I surround myself with like minded people. People who care about the community as much as I do.

My experiences as a poor Trans woman didn't destroy me, if anything they made me stronger and more passionate.

Moving Forward

Sometimes I think back to all the scandals that I encountered and reflect. Why did I survive, when so many of my sisters didn't? What was all the pain and suffering for? What was I searching for during all of this time? While trying to empower and build up my community, in reality I was building and empowering myself. I was and always will be my biggest project.

I gave up prostituting, I'm done . . . hopefully forever! I felt like I was giving up a drug. Still, I was grateful for the opportunities that sex work had given me. I want the next generation of Trans women to feel that they too could do or be anything that they work towards. We don't have to subject ourselves only to sex work. We can still live happy and free by having a job or career that fulfills us.

I moved out of the city and decided to become an author and dedicate my life to education. I feel society needs to get a glimpse of what it's really like to be Trans. Everyone has a story, not many are willing to share it, to say "fuck it all." I'm not living this life in vain.

Living this life, this wonderful, phenomenal life that I've lived, it's still funny to me when I hear people say,
"They chose that life" or "It's the life that they chose."

Let me tell you . . .
I didn't choose this, I was born into this life, this life chose me.
This was the life, the energy that was given to me.

A gift, our lives are a gift.

I had choices of course.

I could've suppressed all of these emotions and feelings and "pretended" to be a "man." I could've gotten married and had children and lived a lie. I could've lived a terribly miserable and unhappy life. I've seen it.

Or I could've just said "fuck it" I can't deal with the battle of my body and mind. I could've just ended this life that was filled with obstacles and struggles that very few get to overcome. I know plenty.

So of course, I looked at this pretty face and said, "bitch you're gonna be a woman." I chose to live life as I felt it was intended.

Regardless of how the whole world perceives me, I'm not ashamed to be a Transsexual, I'm not!

All the shame associated with being Trans is gone. I live unapologetically.
I'm so fuckin proud of the life that I've created for myself. Every experience good or bad has gotten me to this point, right here.

I know that I've made the right choice.
Bitch, "I lived!"

Made in the USA
Monee, IL
28 October 2021

81007607R00069